Drew Provan

iPad

in
easy steps

covers iOS6
for 3rd & 4th generation iPad and iPad 2

In easy steps is an imprint of In Easy Steps Limited
4 Chapel Court · 42 Holly Walk · Leamington Spa
Warwickshire · United Kingdom · CV32 4YS
www.ineasysteps.com

Fourth Edition

Notice of Liability
Every effort has been made to ensure that this book contains accurate
and current information. However, In Easy Steps Limited and the
author shall not be liable for any loss or damage suffered by readers
as a result of any information contained herein.

Trademarks
iOS6® is a registered trademark of Apple Computer, Inc. All other
trademarks are acknowledged as belonging to their respective
companies.

In Easy Steps Limited supports The Forest Stewardship Council (FSC),
the leading international forest certification organisation. All our titles
that are printed on Greenpeace approved FSC certified paper carry the
FSC logo.

MIX
Paper from
responsible sources
FSC® C020837
FSC
www.fsc.org

Printed and bound in the United Kingdom

ISBN 978-1-84078-584-5

Contents

1 Welcome to your new iPad!

The iPad is a multimedia tablet like no other. Its rich graphics and seamless integration with iTunes makes it perfect for work and play. Most tasks requiring a laptop can be carried out on the iPad which is light, power-efficient, instantly-on and incredibly intuitive to use. It also has an huge number of third-party apps to expand its already impressive capabilities.

Welcome to the iPad!

Congratulations on buying an iPad, a sophisticated multimedia tablet computer capable of playing music, dealing with emails, browsing the web, organizing your calendar and thousands of other applications! Or maybe you haven't bought an iPad yet but are considering doing so. Let's look at what you can use the iPad for:

- Listening to music

- Recording and watching videos

- Taking photos

- Reading ebooks

- Browsing the web

- Emails, contacts and calendars

- FaceTime video chats, playing games, and much more

Will it replace my laptop?
Probably not, although for many functions it can be used instead of a laptop. It depends on what you use your laptop for. If you mainly do web browsing, check emails and use social networking apps then the iPad can easily replace your laptop. If, on the other hand, you use your laptop to generate PowerPoint slides or create complex documents then the iPad may not be ideal, since some functions are missing from the iPad.

What's missing from the iPad?
There are features found on laptops and desktops that are missing from the iPad. At present there is no:

- SD card slot

- USB slots (though the Apple Camera Kit does have a 30-pin plug which has a USB socket at one end, but this is to connect your camera rather than attach other devices)

- The ability to access files and drag them around or drop into folders is not available on the iPad. You can get files on there but it's clunky and not very intuitive.

*The term *iPad* is used throughout the book to refer to the "third generation iPad" (originally called "the new iPad") and the "fourth generation iPad" released October 2012.

iPad Specifications

Screen	2048 x 1536 pixels, high resolution, 264 pixels/inch
Weight	652g Wi-Fi model, 662g Wi-Fi + 4G model
Height	241.2 mm
Width	185.7 mm
Depth	9.4 mm
Capacity	16, 32 or 64 GB flash memory
Processor	Dual-core Apple A6X with quad core graphics
Sensors	Three-axis gyro, Accelerometer, Ambient light sensor
TV & Video	AirPlay Mirroring to Apple TV at 720p AirPlay video streaming to Apple TV at up to 1080p at up to 720p Video mirroring and video out support: Up to 720p through Lightning Digital AV Adapter and Lightning to VGA Adapter Video playback up to 1080p
Cameras	iSight (back): 5 megapixels. FaceTime/HD (front): video VGA and VGA still camera
Battery	Built-in 42.5 watt-hour rechargeable. 10 hours web surfing on Wi-Fi 9 hours web surfing using 3G/4G data network
Inputs & Outputs	Lightning Connector port 3.5 mm stereo headphone mini-jack
Built-in speaker	
Microphone	
Micro-SIM card tray (Wi-Fi + 4G models only)	

Hot tip

The table on the left applies to the fourth generation iPad.

You can find the specs of iPad 2 on our website: http://ineasysteps. com/resource-centre/ ipad2spec

Beware

If you have a fourth generation iPad then it'll come with the new lightning connector. You'll need to buy adapters to connect it to your "old" 30-pin accessories, such as TV, iPod dock, etc.

Lightning Connector Adapter

30-pin dock Connector

Lightning Connector

11

What's New in iOS 6?

iOS 6 brings in many new features and apps. The YouTube app has gone but a couple of new apps have arrived — *Find Friends* and *Podcasts*. One major weakness at the time of writing is *Maps*. Previously, mapping data was supplied by Google but the new *Maps* app uses TomTom and the data is currently not up to Apple's usual high standards to say the least!

A quick round-up of the features of iOS 6 is shown below:

Maps

Apple-designed vector-based maps, Turn-by-turn navigation with spoken directions on iPad Wi-Fi + Cellular, Real-time traffic information, Flyover for photo-realistic, interactive 3D views of major metro areas, Siri integration for requesting directions and finding places along a route.

Siri improvements

Sports: scores, player stats, game schedules, team rosters, and league standings for baseball, basketball, football, soccer and hockey, *Movies*: trailers, showtimes, reviews and facts, *Restaurants*: reservations, reviews, photos and information, Send a Tweet, Post on Facebook, App launch.

Facebook integration

Single sign-on from Settings, Post from Photos, Safari, Maps, App Store, iTunes, Game Center, Notification Center and Siri.

Mail improvements

VIP mailbox to access mail from important people quickly, Flagged email mailbox, Insert photos and videos when composing email, Open password protected Office docs, Pull down to refresh mailboxes, Per account signatures.

Safari improvements

iCloud tabs to see open pages on all your devices, Offline Reading List, Photo upload support, Full screen landscape view on iPhone and iPod touch, Smart app banners, JavaScript performance improvements.

App Store and iTunes Store improvements

Updated store design, iTunes Preview history, Complete my season, Complete my album.

Accessibility improvements

Guided Access to limit device to one app or restrict touch input on certain areas of the screen, VoiceOver integration with Maps, AssistiveTouch and Zoom.

Other improvements

- Improved privacy controls for Contacts, Calendars, Reminders, Photos and data shared over Bluetooth

- Reminders can be reordered in the Reminders app

- Custom vibrations for alerts on iPhone

- Clock app for iPad

- Clock alarm with song

- Search all fields in Contacts

- Automatic movie mode for improved video sound quality

- Keyboard shortcuts shared across devices via iCloud

Finding Your Way Around

The physical buttons and controls on the iPad are very simple. Additional functions such as screen brightness are software-controlled.

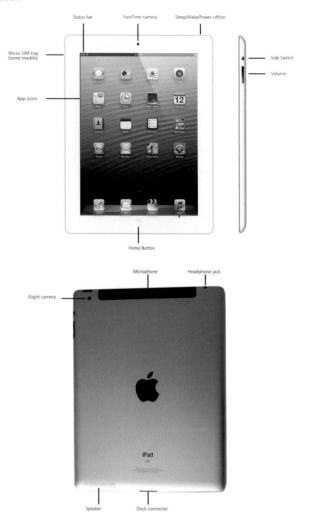

Hot tip

The Multitasking bar is where you will find software controls for Screen Lock, brightness and the Music app

Double-click the Home Button to bring up the Multitasking bar. Slide the Multitasking bar to the right and the software controls for brightness, volume, mirroring, and other functions will appear.

The Nightfly

The **network data icons** at the top of the screen are pretty much like those found on the iPhone.

The fastest data connection is Wi-Fi. If no Wi-Fi is available you will need to use 3G/4G which is fairly fast. Unfortunately, as you move around, the 3G/4G signal will come and go so you may see the 3G/4G disappear and be replaced by the EDGE symbol (E). EDGE is slower than 3G/4G.

If you're *really* unlucky the EDGE signal may vanish and you may see the GPRS symbol. GPRS is *very* slow!

Beware

You must switch off the iPad radios during the flight (see page 64).

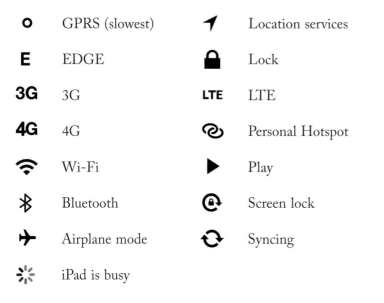

O	GPRS (slowest)	⌐	Location services
E	EDGE	🔒	Lock
3G	3G	**LTE**	LTE
4G	4G	➿	Personal Hotspot
📶	Wi-Fi	▶	Play
✻	Bluetooth	🔒	Screen lock
✈	Airplane mode	↻	Syncing
⁂	iPad is busy		

The GPRS, EDGE and 3G/4G icons are seen on the Wi-Fi + 3G/4G models only.

Home Button & Screen

Hot tip

You can see your active apps by bringing up the Multitasking bar. If an app is misbehaving, quit it using the Multitasking bar.

Hot tip

Another hot tip! To see the Multitasking bar without having to press the Home Button twice, drag four fingers up the screen.

You can also drag four fingers right or left across the screen to switch between running apps.

Beware

What you see when you slide the Multitasking bar to the right (**Mute** or **Screen** Lock) depends on what you have chosen under **Settings > General >Use Side Switch to:**. This iPad has the Side Switch set to lock the screen so the iPad needs to be muted using the software.

There are very few actual physical buttons on the iPad but the Home Button is an important one. The Home Button functions changed since the arrival of iOS 4.2, allowing you to see active apps in the Multitasking bar.

You can now quit active multitasking apps (previously this was not possible with the iPad).

- If you're on the Home Screen (the first screen) it takes you to Search

- If you're on any other screen it takes you right back to the Home Screen and saves you having to flick the screens to the left

- When using the Music application with Home Button it minimizes the Music window allowing you to use other applications while listening to music

- Pressing the Home Button quickly twice brings up the Multitasking bar (shows your active apps) and if you push the Multitasking bar to the right you can see controls for Screen Lock, Brightness, Music, and Volume. AirPlay will only show if you have the latest version of Apple TV (Apple TV 2)

Multitasking bar

The Multitasking bar

Mute   Brightness   Music   Volume
Controls

Slide to right for controls

The **Home Screen** is the first screen you see when you start up the iPad. It contains the apps installed by Apple (and these cannot be deleted). In all, there are 20 of these – 4 will be on the dock.

The dock comes with 4 apps attached. You can move these off, add other apps (the dock can hold a maximum of 6 apps or folders), or you can put your favorite apps there and remove those placed on the dock by Apple.

You can move these apps to other screens if you want to but it's a good idea to keep the most important or most frequently-used apps on this screen.

You might expect iBooks to be a preinstalled app but in fact you have to go to the App Store and download this free app if you want to use the iPad as an ebook reader.

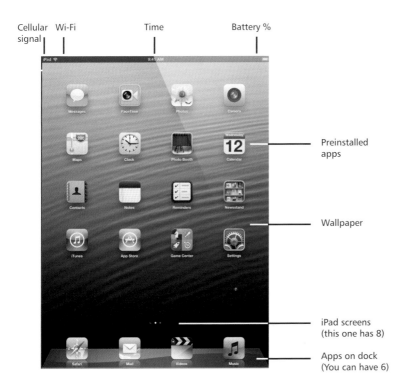

Cellular signal   Wi-Fi   Time   Battery %

Preinstalled apps

Wallpaper

iPad screens (this one has 8)

Apps on dock (You can have 6)

Hot tip

By default there are four apps on the dock at the bottom of the screen. You can add two more if needed.

You can even drag folders to the Dock.

Default Applications

These are the built-in apps.

 Calendar: keeps your appointments in sync with your PC or Mac using wired or wireless sync

 Safari: Apple's home-grown web browser

 Contacts: list of all contacts including phone numbers, email, postal addresses and notes

 Mail: handles IMAP and POP3 email, and syncs to your main accounts on your computer

 Notes: for jotting things down. Sync with your computer or you can email them to yourself

 Photos: show your photos with slideshows or print off photos

 Maps: GPS-enabled maps help you get from A to B, current position, and other information

 Music: controls music, podcasts, etc.

 Videos: play movies and other video content, purchased or from your own collection

 Game Center: social gaming, lets you play games and interact with friends

 iTunes Store: browse and buy music, movies, TV shows and more

 Camera: shoot stills or movies using front or back cameras similar to iPhone functionality

 App Store: your central store for paid and free apps

 FaceTime: video chat to others using iPad, iPhone 4 and 5 or Mac

 Reminders: to-do lists, sync with Apple Mail and Outlook Tasks

 Photo Booth: take still images and select from a series of special effects

 Messages: send SMS-type messages free with Wi-Fi

 Newsstand: stores your newspaper and magazine subscriptions

 Settings: this is where you make changes to personalize your iPad

Two other new apps include Podcasts

and Find Friends

If you don't want these they can be deleted.

The Display & Keyboard

What's all the excitement about the screen? What makes it so special?

The technology behind the multi-touch screen is ingenious. Using one, two, three or four fingers you can do lots of different things on the iPad depending on the app you're using and what you want to do. The main actions are tap, flick, pinch/spread and drag.

The screen is designed to be used with fingers – the skin on glass contact is required (if you tap using your nail you will find it won't work). There are styluses you can buy for the iPad but for full functionality, fingers on screen give the best results.

Tap	Apps open when you tap their icons. Within apps you can select photos, music, web links and many other functions. The tap is similar to a single click with a mouse on the computer
Flick	You can flick through lists like Contacts, Songs, or anywhere there's a long list. Place your finger on the screen and quickly flick up and down and the list scrolls rapidly up and down
Pinch/spread	The iPad screen responds to two fingers placed on its surface. To reduce the size of a photo or web page in Safari place two fingers on the screen and bring them together. To enlarge the image or web page spread your fingers apart and the image grows in size
Drag	You can drag web pages and maps around if you are unable to see the edges. Simply place your finger on the screen and keep it there but move the image or web page around until you can see the hidden areas

Beware

The screen responds best to skin contact. Avoid using pens or other items to tap the screen.

Hot tip

Use four fingers to bring up the Multitasking bar (drag four fingers up the screen), or flick right or left using four fingers to switch between running apps.

...cont'd

The iPad is different to a laptop since there is no physical keyboard. Instead you type by tapping the **virtual keyboard** on the iPad screen itself. You can use the keyboard in portrait or landscape modes. The landscape version provides much wider keys.

The keyboard seems to change in different apps

The keyboard is smart – and should match the app you're in. For example, if you are word processing or entering regular text you will see a standard keyboard. But if you are using a browser or are prompted to enter an email address you will see a modified keyboard with *.com* and @ symbols prominently displayed.

Hot tip

If you have Wi-Fi, try using your voice to dictate emails and other text using the Dictate option (its icon is on the left of the spacebar).

Top left: portrait keyboard in Mail

Top right: portrait keyboard in Pages

Bottom left: portrait keyboard in Safari – note the **Return** key has now changed to **Go**. Tap this to search the web or go to a specific URL

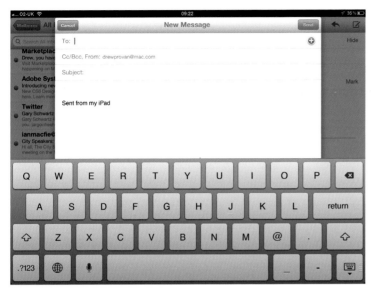

Mail with iPad in the landscape position. Notice how wide the keys have become, making it easier to type without hitting two keys at once! Also notice the Dictation icon to the left of the spacebar (you get this when on Wi-Fi).

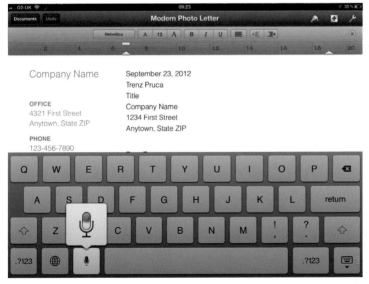

Pages with landscape keyboard. Again, the keyboard is large but the downside is that you lose real estate for work – the effective area for viewing content is quite small. Dictation is active – you can tell because the icon has enlarged and shows the volume level as you dictate your text.

Hot tip

If you find you are making lots of typing errors, try switching the iPad to landscape mode (keys are larger).

21

Caps Lock & Auto-Correct

It's annoying when you want to type something entirely in upper case letters since you have to press Shift for every letter – or do you? Actually, there's a setting which will activate Caps Lock but you need to activate this in settings:

- Go to **Settings**

- Select **General**

- Select **Keyboard**

- Make sure the **Caps Lock** slider is set to **ON**

- While you are there, make sure the other settings are on, for example "." **Shortcut** – this helps you add a period by tapping the spacebar twice (much like the BlackBerry)

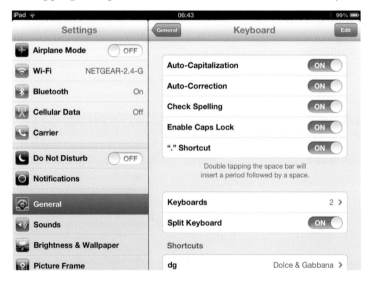

Other settings for the keyboard

- **Auto-Correction** suggests the correct word. If it annoys you, switch it off

- **Auto-Capitalization** is great for putting capitals in names

- The **"." Shortcut** types a period every time you hit the spacebar twice. This saves time when typing long emails but if you prefer not to use this, switch it off. Here's another neat trick – you can also insert a period by tapping the spacebar with two fingers simultaneously

As you type words the iPad **Auto-Correct** will suggest words intelligently which will speed up your typing.

To accept iPad suggestion

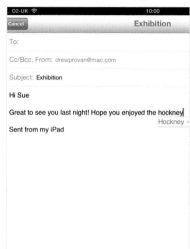

When the suggested word pops up, simply tap the space bar and it will be inserted. The suggested word may not be what you want, in which case you can reject it by tapping the 'x'

To reject suggestion

Above left: iPad will suggest a word but if you don't want to use the suggestion tap the 'x'. The word you type will be added to your user dictionary. Above right: You can look up the dictionary: tap word twice, tap the right arrow and choose Define

All contact names are automatically added to your user dictionary.

Can I Use a Real Keyboard?

There are times when you need real physical keys, for example if you are typing a longer document you might find tapping out your text on the glass screen annoying. Apple has designed a dock with an integrated keyboard, which is great for holding your iPad at the correct angle, and allowing your iPad to be charged while you type using the keyboard.

Original Apple iPad Keyboard and dock (works with the new iPad)

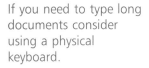

Hot tip

If you need to type long documents consider using a physical keyboard.

ZAGGmate keyboard for iPad 2 (works with the new iPad)

Can I use a Bluetooth keyboard?

Absolutely! The iPad has Bluetooth built-in so you can hook up an Apple Bluetooth keyboard and type away. Alternatively, there are third-party keyboards such as the ZAGGmate Bluetooth keyboard (*www.zagg.com*) which acts as a case when not in use (protects the front of the iPad but not the back).

Keyboard Tricks

Although it's not immediately obvious, the keyboard can generate accents, acutes, and many other foreign characters and symbols.

Holding the letter "u" or "e" generates lots of variants. Just slide your finger along till you reach the one you want and it will be inserted into the document.

Hot tip

For accents and other additional characters, touch the key then slide your finger to the character you want to use.

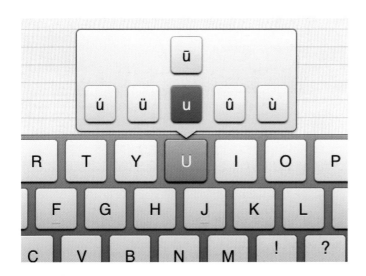

Also, when you use Safari you don't have to enter ".co.uk" in URLs — the ".com" key will produce other endings if you touch and hold the key.

Select, Copy & Paste Text

Rather than retype text, you can select text (or pictures) and paste these into other documents or the URL field in Safari. Touch and hold text, images or URL (links) to open, save or copy them.

To select text

Touch and hold a paragraph of text to select. Drag the blue handles to enclose the text you want to copy then tap **Copy**

Copy web links by tapping and selecting **Copy**. If you just want to go to the site click **Open** in New Tab

Use the built-in dictionary by tapping a word then Define

Paste copied text or images by tapping screen in e.g., Pages

Making Corrections

Sometimes words get mistyped. You could retype the whole word but it's easier to correct. Since the iPad isn't a laptop there is no mouse and pointer so you need to get the cursor next to the incorrect character. You can then delete that character and replace it with the correct character.

To position the cursor where you want it

1 Put your finger onto the incorrect word (you may need to tap and hold)

2 Keep your finger on the screen and slide your finger along the word until the cursor is just ahead of the incorrect letter(s)

3 Backspace (delete from right to left) and delete the incorrect character

4 Insert the correct character(s) then locate the end of your text and tap the screen to position the cursor at the end so you can start typing again

5 The iPad can help you if you don't know how to spell the word (tap **Replace...** and it will suggest some words

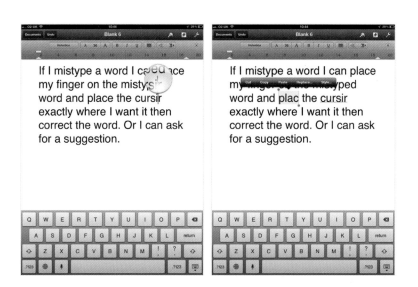

Hot tip

You can also correct by double-tapping the incorrectly spelled word and choosing **Replace** then selecting the correct word.

Finding Things on the iPad

Sometimes you haven't got time to look through your entire calendar for an appointment, or to scroll through iTunes for one track. You can use Spotlight (Apple's indexing and search facility) to find specific apps, contacts, emails, appointments and Music content.

Start search

Hot tip

Search using Spotlight to avoid spending ages looking for emails, music tracks and other data.

1 From the Home Screen press the Home Button (if you are away from the Home Screen, press the Home Button twice)

2 You will be taken to the Spotlight search screen (this is one screen to the *left* of the Home Screen)

3 Enter your search word or string into the search box

4 Your results will show up below. The results are grouped according to their type, i.e. Calendar appointment, email, etc.

Hot tip

To reach Spotlight from the Home Screen press the Home Button once. To get to Spotlight from any other screen press the Home Button twice.

The word "Design" shows up in

Contacts

One app

An iPod track

One email

One appointment

You can choose to search the web or Wikipedia

Enter search term here

Making Folders

You will accumulate lots of free and paid apps which will occupy several iPad screens. When you have many apps it can be difficult finding the one you want since you have to flick across several screens to find the right one.

Apple has made it easier to organize your apps by providing the option of creating folders. You might want a folder for games, one for social networking, serious work, and other activities.

Creating a folder

1. **Hold an app** until all the apps start jiggling on the screen (you will see a small circle on the top left with an **x** – tap the **x** to delete the app)

2. To create a games folder, **touch and hold** a games app and **drag it** onto another games app. One will disappear into the other and a folder will be created with the name *Games*. Rename it if you want to

3. Do this for all the folders you want to create then tap the Home Button. This stops the apps jiggling

Don't forget

You don't need to accept the folder name chosen by the iPad – rename it to whatever you want.

Dragging one app onto another has created a folder called Lifestyle

Here are the contents of the Games folder. To close the folder, tap outside the folder

Multitasking

The iPad can run several programs at once. To see the apps that are loaded you need to reveal the Multitasking bar at the bottom of the screen. If you want to, you can quit one or more apps and free up some memory (whether this is needed is debatable, but the opportunity is there if you want to use it).

How to quit running apps

1 Tap the **Home Button** twice – the Multitasking bar will appear at the bottom of the screen

2 Touch and hold **one app** until they start jiggling – you will see a red icon with a white line in the center at the top left of each running app

3 To quit the app, tap the **red icon**

4 When finished, tap the **Home Button** twice

Tapping the Home Button twice brings up the Multitasking bar. There are 5 apps running

Touch and hold then quit any of the running apps

2 Getting Started

As with all technology, although the iPad is plug-and-play, there is some initial setting up to do. It's worth spending some time setting up the iPad so it suits your needs.

Turn the iPad On & Register

You can put your iPad fully off or into sleep mode (sleep mode is useful because as soon as you press the Home Button the iPad is instantly on).

Hot tip

Use sleep mode to put your iPad off unless you are not planning to use it for an extended period.

- If the iPad is fully off, press and hold the **On/Off button**. The iPad will boot up

- When you have finished using it simply press the **On/Off button** briefly and the iPad will enter sleep mode again

- Sleep mode uses very little power so for the sake of speed simply use sleep mode unless you are not going to use the iPad for several days

- To wake from sleep, press the **Home Button** or **On/Off switch**

To fully power off

1 Press and hold the **On/Off** switch until you see the slider bar and **Slide to Power Off** appears

2 Slide the red slider to the right

3 The iPad will fully shut down

Lock the screen

The iPad works in portrait (upright) and landscape (sideways) modes. The iPad is clever and can tell which way up it is being held and the screen will rotate accordingly. Sometimes you will want it to stay fixed in portrait or landscape modes.

Hot tip

You can configure the Side Switch to lock the screen in portrait or landscape mode by choosing **General settings > Use Side Switch to: Lock Rotation or Mute.**

To do this, lock the screen:

The Screen Lock is controlled by software. You need to activate the **Multitasking bar** (press **Home Button** twice), then slide it to the right to reveal the **Screen Lock** control

Tap the **Screen Lock icon** (extreme left) to lock the screen

Like the iPhone, the iPad needs to be **registered** with Apple before you can use it.

To register

1 Plug the iPad into your computer (Mac or PC) using the sync cable provided. iTunes should open automatically. If not double-click the app to **launch iTunes** manually

2 The Devices tab on the right side of the iTunes window should show the **iPad**. You will then see the **Welcome to Your New iPad** pane in iTunes

3 Click **Continue** to reach the next screen

4 **Accept the license conditions** and click **Continue**

5 The next pane requests your iTunes account ID and password. If you do not have an iTunes account click the **I do not have an Apple ID** option. Click **Continue**

6 The next page will ask if you want to use iCloud for Push Email/Calendar and Contacts

7 Either choose to use your existing iCloud account, or register for one, or if you don't want iCloud select **Not Now**

8 The next pane lets you **name** your iPad and decide how you want to sync your data (songs, videos, and other content) to the iPad

9 If you want songs and videos to sync automatically check the boxes marked **Automatically Sync Songs and Videos to My iPad**, **Automatically Add Photos to my iPad**, and **Automatically Sync Applications to my iPad**

Sync Your Data

Your iPad can store several types of information:

- Calendar
- Email
- Contacts
- Music
- Photos
- Videos
- Podcasts
- Apps (applications, i.e. programs)
- Documents
- Other content

This information will mainly reside on your computer. You will need to decide which music, photos, videos and other content get synced to the iPad.

You are unlikely to want to sync *all* of your media because the iPad storage capacity is limited, and will be less than your computer.

You will need to choose which media files and apps get synced when you plug your iPad into your computer.

- You can opt *not* to open iTunes automatically when you plug the iPad in
- You can also choose to sync your data *manually* rather than automatically

The Info pane shows 5 main boxes on the screen:

- Sync Address Book Contacts
- Sync iCal Calendars
- Sync Mail Accounts
- Other – Sync Notes
- Advanced – Replace Information on this iPad Contacts/Calendars/Mail Accounts/Notes

Hot tip

Automated syncs take the guesswork out of syncing.

Sync your contacts

- If you want all of your contacts currently on your computer to sync with the iPad check the radio button **All Contacts**

- If you *don't* want all your contacts but maybe just family and friends click **Selected Groups** and select those you wish to sync

- Next time you plug the iPad in those contacts will sync, or you can click the **Sync** button at the bottom right of the iTunes window

Sync iCal calendars

iCal allows you to have multiple calendars (so, too, does Microsoft Outlook), for example, home, work, vacation, etc.

- If you want to sync *all* of your calendars check the **All Calendars** radio button

- If you only want some calendar data synced, check the **Selected Calendars** button and go through your calendar list to choose those you want synced

Sync mail accounts

You may have multiple email accounts and you can choose whether to sync them all or just selected account.

- Select **All** or **Selected Mail Accounts**

Other

- Select whether to **sync Safari bookmarks** (makes Safari on the iPad and computer show identical bookmarks)

- You can also select the **Sync Notes** radio button if you want your Notes (found within Mail on the Mac, or Outlook on the PC) to sync to the iPad

Advanced pane

This lets you **Replace All Contacts, Calendars, Mail Accounts and Notes** on the iPad with data from the computer.

...cont'd

Apple iCloud

This is a service that allows you to use the cloud to sync your data (calendars, contacts, mail, Safari bookmarks, and notes) wirelessly.

Once you are registered and set up, any entries or deletions to calendars and other apps are reflected in all devices using iCloud.

Register for an iCloud account

Go to *www.apple.com/icloud/setup*

Start using iCloud on the iPad and computers

1. Plug the iPad into your computer

2. In the iTunes **Info pane** make sure the sync buttons for Contacts, Calendars, Mail accounts are *not* checked

3. Open the iCloud System Preferences (Mac) or Control Panel (PC)

4. Log into your iCloud account (you only need to do this once – it will remember your name and password)

5. Under the **Sync** tab, select the items you want to sync between the computer and the iPad. If you want to sync **automatically** check that radio button (or you may choose to sync every hour, day, week, or manually). The automatic sync is the simplest option

6. From now, all changes made to calendars, contacts, Safari bookmarks and other data on the iPad will be reflected on the equivalent programs on your computer

Set up your iCloud account to sync the things you want

Find my Mac

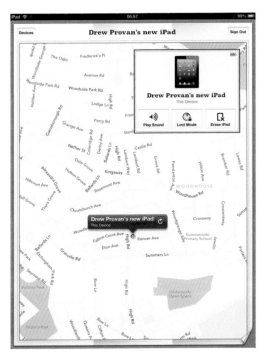

This is a great feature which allows you to see where your devices are. Once activated, (**Settings > iCloud > Find my iPad**), log into iCloud using a browser and click Find My iPhone. This will find your iPad and any other devices you have registered.

...cont'd

Get Your Calendar in Sync

The iPad can sync its calendar with iCal (Mac), Microsoft Outlook (PC), and Google Calendar.

- Connecting the iPad to the computer will sync all calendar events if you have chosen this sync method (click the radio button in the **Info** pane) or you can sync using iCloud or Exchange

- If you have multiple calendars you can choose to sync specific calendars

On the Mac you are able to sync calendars with multiple applications but on the PC you can only sync with one application at a time.

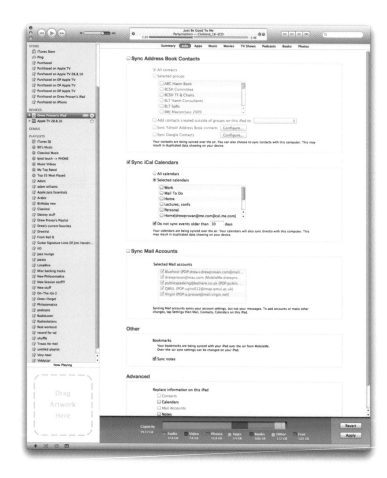

Syncing other Data

Syncing contacts

Again, you can choose the wired route or wireless using iCloud.

1. Under the **Info** pane in iTunes (with the iPad plugged in!) select the method of sync and decide which contacts you want to sync

2. You can choose to sync **All Contacts** or **Selected Groups**

3. You can also sync your Yahoo! and Google contacts if you have these accounts. Click the **Configure button** for any of these services if you use them

On the PC, contacts can sync with Microsoft Outlook, Google Contacts, Windows Address Book and Yahoo! Address Book.

Hot tip

Your calendar and contacts list are more likely to be up-to-date if you choose a wireless sync method.

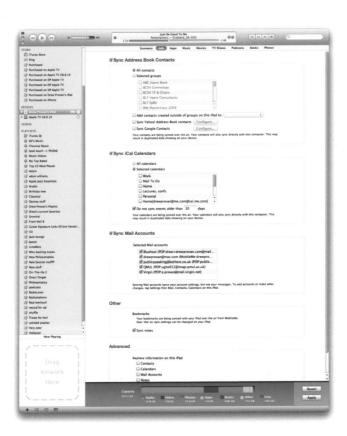

...cont'd

Sync Mail

Mail can be synced using the wired route or wirelessly using iCloud. You will need to decide which method works best for you.

1. For wired sync, plug your iPad into the computer and select the **Info** pane in iTunes

2. Click the **Sync Mail Accounts** button

3. Choose which accounts you wish to sync. This syncs your email settings but does *not* sync the actual email messages themselves

4. If using the wireless iCloud route, leave the **Sync Mail Settings** button unchecked

5. Open the **iCloud System Preferences** (Mac) or **Control Panel** (PC)

6. Check the **Mail Accounts** radio button if you want to sync the account settings

7. On the Mac, the iPad mail syncs to Apple Mail. On the PC, the iPad mail syncs with Microsoft Outlook

8. The account settings are synced from computer to iPad

Beware

Changes made to the Mail settings on the iPad will not be synced back to the computer.

Sync apps

This is useful so that you have a backup of the apps in case you need to restore the iPad.

1 Click the **Apps** pane in iTunes when the iPad is connected to your computer

2 Click the **Sync Apps** radio button if you want to sync your apps. On the left side you will see a list of all the available apps

3 On the right side you will see a mini-representation of all the screens on your iPad with the apps in their positions on the screens

4 Click the **radio button** for all the apps you want to sync. Leave unchecked those apps you do not want to copy to the iPad

5 Use the mini screen windows to move your apps to wherever you want to place them (you can do this on the iPad, too, but it is much easier on the computer)

6 Click the **Sync** button at the bottom right of the iTunes window to sync the apps between iPad and computer

Hot tip

To move lots of apps it's much easier to use the mini-screens in iTunes on the computer than it is to do this on the iPad itself, as shown on the left.

...cont'd

Sync music

1   Select the **Music** pane in iTunes

2   Click the **Sync Music button** if you want to sync music from the computer to your iPad

3   Leave this button unchecked if you don't want to sync music to your iPad

The available storage on your iPad is limited so the chances are you will not be able to sync all your music across to the iPad. The best thing to do is create smart playlists (see Music section).

You could choose only to sync specific **Artists**, **Genres**, or **Albums** by checking the appropriate radio buttons.

Beware

Leave enough memory on the iPad for apps and other files. Don't fill the entire memory capacity with music!

If All Your Music Won't Fit

Most of us have more music than will fit on the iPad (you need to leave *some* storage space for apps, docs and other items) and Apple has devised clever ways of allowing us to sync only selected content.

● If your music library in iTunes is small you can probably choose to sync **Entire Music Library**

● You can choose whether to copy music videos and voice memos by checking their radio buttons

● You can also allow your computer to fill all the available space on the iPad with songs but that will leave no free room for more apps and other files. It's probably best not to choose this option

Hot tip

Syncing your music is much easier if you create Playlists and Hot Playlists.

Make life easier using playlists

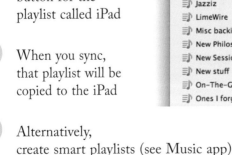

1 Make yourself a playlist in iTunes (call it *iPad*)

2 Drag the tracks you want on the iPad onto this playlist folder

3 Under the **Music pane** in iTunes check the radio button for the playlist called iPad

4 When you sync, that playlist will be copied to the iPad

5 Alternatively, create smart playlists (see Music app)

PLAYLISTS
- iTunes DJ
- 60's Music
- Classical Music
- Ipod touch -> PHONE
- Music Videos
- My Top Rated
- Top 25 Most Played
- Adam
- adam williams
- Apple Jazz Essentials
- Arabic
- Birthday new
- Classical
- Dancey stuff
- Drew Provan's Playlist
- Drew's current favorites
- DrewVal
- From Neil B
- Guitar Signature Licks Of Jimi Hendri...
- iiO
- Jazz lounge
- Jazziz
- LimeWire
- Misc backing tracks
- New Philosomatkia
- New Session stuff??
- New stuff
- On-The-Go 2
- Ones I forget

Sync Videos

You will no doubt want to watch videos on your iPad. You can buy these from iTunes directly on the iPad, or on computer or Apple TV. You can also sync your own DVDs onto the iPad.

1 Connect the iPad to the computer and open iTunes

2 Click the **Movies** pane in iTunes

3 You can sync the **10 Most Recent Movies** to the iPad, or you can sync **Selected** movies

4 View your available movies in iTunes and click radio buttons for all those you wish to transfer to the iPad

5 Click **Sync**

6 To remove the selected movies from the iPad you need to *uncheck* their radio boxes in iTunes and **Click Sync**. The movie you have deselected will then be removed from the iPad

Beware

Video files are fairly large so try not to have too many videos on your iPad at one time.

Sync TV Shows

You can buy TV shows using iTunes on your iPad, computer or Apple TV. If you purchase TV shows on your computer you can choose to sync those to the iPad. If you buy TV shows on the iPad they will sync to your computer.

① Connect the iPad to the computer

② In iTunes select **TV Shows**

③ Click **Sync TV Shows** if you want to copy these to your iPad

You can copy only **Unwatched** TV shows, or **Newest, Newest Unwatched, 3 Newest,** and various other options.

By checking individual radio buttons for TV shows you can choose precisely which content gets synced to the iPad.

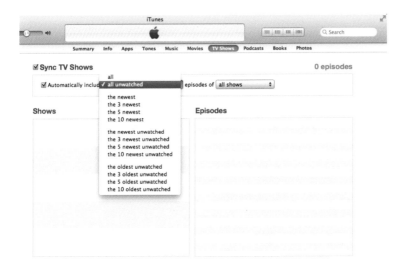

Sync Podcasts

You can subscribe to podcasts using your computer (using iTunes Store) or the iPad.

To sync podcasts to the iPad

1 Connect the iPad to the computer

2 Open the iTunes **Podcasts** pane

3 Select to sync all podcasts automatically or choose specific podcasts

4 To remove podcasts from the iPad, uncheck their buttons in iTunes and sync – the selected podcasts will be removed from the iPad

Sync Books

You can buy books from the iBooks Store on the iPad (many are free!) or using your computer.

Sync books to the iPad

1 Connect the iPad to the computer

2 Open the **Books** pane in iTunes

3 Select to sync **All Books** or **Selected Books**

4 Check the radio button for those you want to sync to the iPad

5 To remove, uncheck their radio buttons in the iTunes **Books** pane and those deselected will be removed during the next sync

Syncing Your Photos

You will want to have photos from your computer copied across to the iPad. This is very straightforward.

On the Mac, photos can be chosen from iPhoto or Aperture. On the PC you can sync your photos from Adobe Photoshop Album or Adobe Photoshop Elements. Alternatively, you can sync photos with any folder on your computer that contains photos.

1. Select the Photos pane in iTunes

2. Choose the application or the folder on your computer containing photos

3. Select **Specific Albums,** or **Events**, or **Faces**

4. Check all those you want to sync and click **Sync**

5. To remove, uncheck their boxes and at the next sync they will be removed

Getting the iPad Online

The iPad is a fun device for listening to music, watching videos and playing games but to experience the full potential you need to get it online.

Getting online

The fastest connection is Wi-Fi. All iPad models include the Wi-Fi receiver which means you can browse available wireless networks, choose one and connect.

1 Select **Settings > Wi-Fi**

2 Slide the Wi-Fi slider to **On** if it is Off

3 A list of available wireless networks will appear under **Choose a Network.** Tap the one you want to connect to

4 You will likely be prompted for a username and password since most networks are locked (if the network is *open* you will get straight on)

5 Check the signal strength indicator which will give you an idea of how strong the signal is

Join networks automatically

If this setting is selected your iPad will connect automatically to wireless networks. This is useful if you move from place to place and have previously joined their network – you will not be prompted each time to re-enter your details. But if you don't want the iPad to join networks automatically, switch this off.

- Sometimes you don't want the iPad to remember all used networks (hotels, airports, etc.)

- Go to **Settings > Wi-Fi** and the select the network you want the iPad to forget

- Click the right arrow

- Tap **Forget this Network** and it will be deleted from the list

Beware

The iPad may join networks that you don't particularly want to join. Tell it to forget certain networks.

The Preinstalled Apps

Calendar

This app keeps you organized. It is similar to iCal on the Mac and Outlook on the PC. The interface is beautiful and it's very easy to enter your appointment details. Usefully, the app's icon (before you click it to open the app) shows the current date.

You can sync your events (appointments) from the Mac or PC using either the wired or wireless (iCloud) routes.

The Calendar app will be explored more fully in a later chapter.

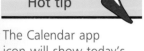

Hot tip

The Calendar app icon will show today's date even when not launched, which is very useful.

Contacts

This app stores the details of all your contacts. Contacts resembles a physical address book with left and right facing pages.

The app works in both portrait and landscape modes.

You can view contacts, add, edit and delete. If you want to add a photo to a contact this is very easy.

There is smooth integration with Address Book on the Mac and Outlook on the PC.

Notification Center

As well as messages popping up on your screen from Facebook, SMS, etc. you can also see all your notifications including anniversaries and other appointments using the Notification screen. From any screen simply swipe your finger down the screen and all your notifications will appear.

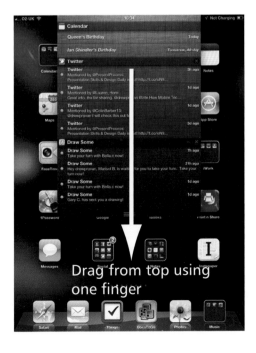

Mail app

Mail is the powerhouse for managing all your email. The Mail app can handle multiple accounts, POP3, IMAP and Exchange. The emails are easy to read and HTML is handled well. The app's views vary depending on whether you hold the iPad in portrait or landscape modes.

Mail closely resembles Mail on the Mac although there are some limitations such as the handling of signatures (you cannot have multiple signatures on the iPad version, for example).

Hot tip

Some people say they prefer non-HTML email, but HTML email looks much nicer than plain email.

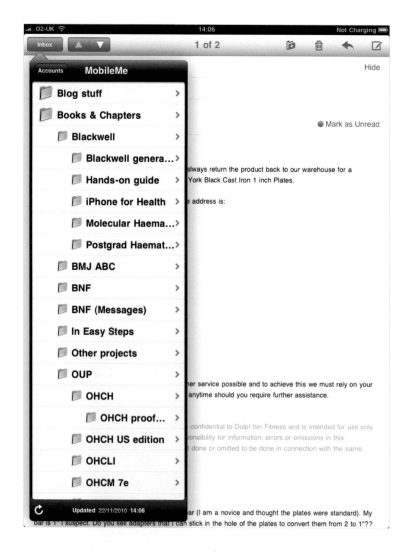

Notes app

This is very similar to Notes on the iPhone although the interface is easier to use. You can scroll through a list of notes, add new notes, edit, and share using email. You can also sync your notes from the iPad with the Mac (using Apple Mail) and PC (Outlook).

If you find Notes too limiting you can always view the huge variety of third-party apps on the App Store, or you could try a web-based notes service such as Remember The Milk (*rememberthemilk.com*) or Google tasks.

Newsstand

If you subscribe to newspapers or magazines this new app is where they will end up. Tap the app and browse through your subscriptions.

Videos app

The iPad is a gorgeous multimedia device. Its large, high-resolution screen makes videos a joy to watch. Unlike the iPhone and iPod there is a separate Videos app.

You can watch music videos, movies rented or bought from iTunes or you can copy your own movies across. Plug in a decent pair of headphones and immerse yourself!

Getting your own movies onto the iPad is very easy (this is covered later in the book).

Messages

iMessages from your iPhone and Mac can now be synced with the iPad. All of your devices should show the same messages (much like Skype does).

iMessage on iPhone (above) shows on iPad too!

Reminders

The Reminders app on iOS devices is a welcome addition. The interface is simple and easy to use.

Reminders

Geotagging

Because the iPad uses Geotagging data it knows where you are. You can set up Reminders that notify you when you are in a specific location based on Geotagging data. At the time of writing, location-based reminders work well on iPhone but the feature is flaky on iPad (many people including me cannot get location-based reminders to work but an update to iOS 6 should fix this).

...cont'd

Settings app

The Settings app is the central hub for controlling all aspects of your iPad. It is the equivalent to System Preferences on your Mac or Control Panels on the PC. We will explore this in greater detail in a later chapter.

Use settings for:

- Activating Airplane mode

- Connecting to Wi-Fi

- Setting notifications for individual apps

- Review cellular data usage

- Adjusting the brightness of the screen, and choosing wallpaper

- Setting up Mail, Calendars and Contacts

- Controlling audio, Music, Safari

- Configuring FaceTime

Don't forget

The Settings app allows you to customize the iPad to suit your specific needs.

Safari app

Although you can download third party browsers from the App Store, Safari is the preinstalled browser on the iPad. It is fast, clean and easy to use. It is very similar to its big brother on the Mac and PC.

You can open several browser windows at the same time and toggle between them.

Bookmarks

You can keep these in sync with Safari on your computer using either iCloud or iTunes.

Safari has an unobtrusive search box for Google which you can switch to Yahoo! or Bing if you prefer.

Hot tip

If you don't want Google as your search engine – change it to Yahoo! or Bing.

...cont'd

Photos app

Visually stunning, the Photos app is perfect for showing off your photos. You can review by Photos or Albums and play slideshows. There is also an option to email specific photos. You can also show off your photos using the Picture Frame feature on the iPad, where you use your iPad as a digital photo frame.

This shows the Lock Screen. Instead of sliding the slider to the right to access the iPad, tap the Picture Frame icon (bottom right, showing a flower motif) and you will see your pictures displayed at full screen. The pictures will change every few seconds

Launching Photos will bring up your photo collection which you can browse in a number of ways – Photos, Albums, Events, Faces or Places

Music app

The Music app on the iPad is very similar to the conventional iPod but because the screen real estate is so large, you can view albums and their covers at a larger size, in all their glory! The layout of the screens is very clear, and you can select your music from playlists, albums, artists and several other ways. The functionality is much better than the iPod or iPhone.

Using playlists and smart playlists you can gain complete control over the content you sync to the iPad.

...cont'd

FaceTime app

There was no
FaceTime with the
original iPad because
FaceTime requires a
camera, something
that was missing
from iPad 1. Now
with iPad 2 and the
new iPad we have

Image courtesy of Apple

the front camera which is perfect for video chatting. The rear camera
is also useful for showing your caller what you are looking at.

What do you need?

1. iPad with FaceTime and a Wi-Fi connection

2. Other person needs FaceTime on their iPhone, iPad , or
   Mac (previously Wi-Fi only but now works with 3G/4G
   connections)

3. Apple ID (i.e. iTunes account, iCloud)

Using FaceTime

1. Launch **FaceTime**

2. **Sign in** if not already signed in (you don't need to do
   this each time)

3. Tap **Contacts** and find the person you want to
   FaceTime chat with

4. Tap their **email address** or cell phone number (the
   latter will start a FaceTime call using their iPhone

5. Add to favorites if you plan to call this person regularly

6. Tap **Recents** to return a recent FaceTime call

Photo Booth

As the name suggests, this app lets you take photos of yourself as
if you were in a photo booth. It also has several built-in effects
which distort the image.

1   Launch **Photo Booth**

2   Choose the effect you want to
    use, e.g. Thermal Camera, X-ray
    etc. If you want a standard
    image choose Normal

3   Tap the **shutter button**
    at the bottom and the Photo
    Booth will take a picture which
    will be added to your
    camera roll

Find Friends

So long as you're not prone to paranoia you can allow your friends
to track your location. This way, they can keep track of your
movements. I track a couple of friends but don't allow them to see
my location.

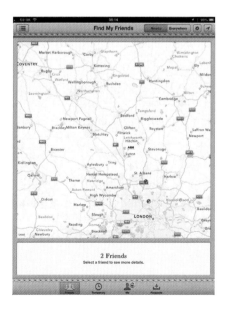

Restore and Reset the iPad

Your entire iPad contents will be backed up every time you sync with your computer – iTunes takes care of this. For that reason, you should perform regular syncs with your computer, even if you don't want to update the content.

If the iPad misbehaves and you need to restore it you will need a recent backup file to use for the restore.

Restoring the iPad erases the iPad and copies all of your apps, settings, and data from the restore file which iTunes will have created for you (*providing you have synced recently!*).

To restore iPad

1 Connect the iPad to the computer

2 Make sure iTunes is open and select your iPad when it appears in iTunes under **Devices**

3 Select the **Summary** tab

4 Select the **Restore** option

5 When prompted to back up your settings before restoring, select the **Back Up** option. If you have performed a recent backup you can ignore this

Resetting the iPad

If you have an iPhone you may be familiar with the reset option.

1 Hold down the **Home Button + On/Off** button for several seconds

2 The screen will go black and the Apple logo will appear on the screen

3 Let go of the buttons now

The iPad should boot up. Any problems you had before should have been corrected. If not, try **restoring** the iPad.

Don't forget

Back up your iPad regularly so you have a recent backup with which to perform a restore if things go badly wrong!

Hot tip

Reset the iPad if it misbehaves.

3 iPad Settings

The whole look and feel of the iPad is controlled through Settings, one of the apps preinstalled on the iPad. In this section we will look at all settings, from wallpapers to the Music app, getting things set up perfectly for optimal use.

Up in the Air

The iPad is a great multimedia device for listening to music or watching movies on the plane. There are strict rules about wireless and cellular receivers – these must be switched off during the flight. Airplane Mode switches all iPad radios off. Airplane mode is only seen with the Wi-Fi + 4G models.

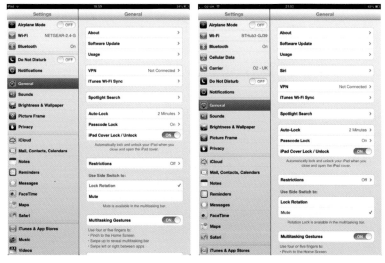

Settings on Wi-Fi model   Settings on Wi-Fi + 4G model

Wi-Fi only models

 Go to **Settings > Wi-Fi**. Turn Wi-Fi **OFF** by tapping the On/Off button or sliding the slider to the right

Wi-Fi is now fully off. You cannot receive Wi-Fi signals and the iPad is safe to use on the plane

Wi-Fi + 4G models

Go to **Settings > Airplane Mode** and push the slider to the right

Wi-Fi and 4G radios are now fully off

For both models, when you are off the plane, go back to settings and slide the slider to the left which switches the radios back on.

Getting online with Wi-Fi

The iPad is designed to be used online – using either a wireless connection or 4G (slower). You can use it without Internet access but you won't be able to browse online content, download apps, content, or update your apps.

Connect to a wireless network

1 Open **Settings > Wi-Fi**

2 Make sure Wi-Fi is set to **ON**

3 Choose a network: you will see a list of available networks near you. If locked (most are) you will see a padlock symbol. Some networks may appear "open" and let you connect but when you browse you will be presented with a request for username and password

4 Tap the name of the network you want to connect to

5 Enter the password if you know it

6 You should see a check mark next to the network name showing which wireless network you have joined

7 If your network is hidden but you know its name tap **Other...**

8 You can allow the iPad to join networks quietly without alerting you (**Ask to Join Networks OFF**) or you may prefer to be asked before the iPad joins a network (**Ask to Join Networks ON**)

Hot tip

No Wi-Fi connection? If you have an iPhone, switch on Personal Hotspot (Settings > Personal Hotspot). This lets the iPad use the iPhone's 3G/4G connection. Be careful – the data used comes out of your iPhone allowance!

...cont'd

9 You can see the strength of the connection by checking the wireless icon at the top left of the iPad display or in the wireless connection window (in **Settings**)

Setting network connection manually

1 Tap the blue arrow to the right of the network name

2 You can choose an IP Address using **DHCP**, **BootIP**, or **Static Address. Subnet Mask, Router, DNS**, and **Search Domains** are also shown in the window though you won't need to change these

3 If you use a proxy to get onto the Internet, enter the details manually or set to **Auto**. Most people don't use proxies so it is unlikely you'll need to change anything here

Settings on Wi-Fi + 4G model

Setting up Notifications

If you have used the iPhone you will be familiar with notifications. These are audio and visual alerts used by some apps. For example, if you use a messaging app you may want to see how many unread messages there are without actually opening the app. Or, if you use an app like Skype, you may want to be shown on screen when someone is calling you even when the iPad screen is locked. By setting up your notifications you can choose how much or how little information you receive in terms of messages, calls, updates, etc.

Set up notifications

1 Open **Settings > Notifications**

2 Switch Notifications to **ON**

3 You will see a list of apps that use Notifications

4 To configure Notifications for an app, tap its name in the list

Some apps offer notification by **Sounds, Alerts** and **Badges**. Sounds **ON** means the iPad will play a sound when a notification is received. Alerts are messages that display on the screen, and Badges are the red circles that appear at the top right of the app's icon when notifications have been received.

Hot tip

Spend some time setting up your Notifications to avoid unwanted intrusions by apps sending useless notifications!

If you want to keep intrusion from notifications to a minimum, switch off Notifications completely or adjust the settings on an app-by-app basis.

Cellular Data

This is only shown in the Wi-Fi model.

Check cellular data

 1   Go to **Settings** > **Cellular Data**

2   Make sure Cellular Data is **ON**

You may want to use **Data Roaming** to get online if you are away from your home country. *Note*: roaming charges for Internet access are high so be careful if you switch this to ON. In general, it is better to leave this switched OFF!

- You can view your account, review your data plan, **Add Data** or **Change Plan** (from pay-as-you-go to monthly), and Edit User Information

- **APN Settings** will vary depending on your carrier

- You can set up a **SIM PIN**

- Under **SIM Applications** you will see lots of services provided by your 3G/4G carrier

Beware

When abroad, keep Data Roaming OFF or your phone bill may be huge – the cost of data download outside your own country is generally very high. Or you may be very wealthy in which case you can switch it on!

Set up Your Wallpaper

Just like your Mac or PC, you can change the picture displayed at the Lock Screen and the background you see behind the apps. You can alter both of these using the in-built iPad wallpapers or you can use your own pictures.

Apple has already provided some excellent images but you may want more. There are several websites offering wallpapers and one of the best is *interfacelift.com* which offers stunning photos for Mac and PC – these should work on the iPad as well.

Changing the wallpaper

1   Go to **Settings > Wallpaper**

2   Choose the options on the screen or tap **>** to scroll to the right for other pictures

3   From the next window select **Wallpaper** (inbuilt iPad pictures) or **Saved Photos**, from your own photo collection on the iPad

4   Tap to make your choice and decide whether you want the new image as only wallpaper or Lock Screen or both

Use Apple wallpapers or your own photos

Saved photos available for use as wallpaper

The iPad as a Picture Frame

You can use the photos on your iPad for more than just wallpaper – the iPad can be used as an (expensive) electronic picture frame, displaying your photos in an ever-changing display.

Activating Picture Frame

1 From the **Lock Screen**, instead of entering your PIN when you wake the iPad up, tap the bottom right **Picture Frame icon**

2 The iPad will display your pictures in sequence, the duration of which can be changed using the settings

3 Go to **Settings > Picture Frame**

4 Choose **Transition — Dissolve** or **Origami**

5 You can set the iPad to **Zoom** in on **Faces**

6 If you want to shuffle the order, switch **Shuffle** to **ON**

7 You can choose to display **All Photos** or choose specific **Albums**

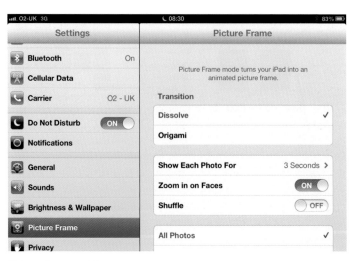

Picture frame settings

General Settings

About
This provides full information about your iPad, serial number, number of apps installed, songs, and much more.

Usage
This tells you how much data you have sent and received. You can also switch Battery Percentage on here.

Sounds
You can configure the alert sounds for New Mail arriving, Sent Mail, Calendar Alerts, Lock Sounds and Keyboard Clicks.

Network
Lets you see your VPN (Virtual Private Network) connection if you use one, or the wireless network to which you are connected.

Bluetooth
This lets you switch the Bluetooth radio on and off.

Spotlight Search
Determines the types of items that appear in the Spotlight Search window.

Location Services
Some apps like to know where you are (Maps, Google Earth, and many others). You will need to switch Location Services ON to allow your location to be determined.

Autolock
This locks the screen if there is no input after a set period. You can select between 2–15 minutes or Never. Something around five minutes is probably the most practical. Once the autolock is activated you will need to re-enter your four-digit PIN at the Lock Screen to use the iPad.

...cont'd

Hot tip

Passcode Lock prevents people accessing your iPad and its data!

Passcode Lock

You don't need to set this but your data will be safer if you switch this to ON. Set a four-digit PIN that you will remember!

iPad Cover Lock/ Unlock

Lets you lock screen when not in use.

Restrictions

Useful if the iPad will be used by children. You can limit access to apps such as Safari, YouTube, and iTunes. You can also prohibit the installation of apps.

Use Side Switch to:

You can configure the Side Switch to lock rotation, or activate the Mute function.

Multitasking Gestures

This setting allows you to pinch to activate the Home Screen, swipe up (four fingers) to reveal the Multitasking bar, or swipe left or right between running apps.

Date & Time

Choose the 12- or 24-hour clock. Set Time Zone, Date and Time.

Keyboard

Here you can enable and disable Auto-Correction, Auto-Capitalization of the first word in sentences, Enable Caps Lock and "." Shortcut (two taps on spacebar generates a period).

Settings > General > Keyboard > International Keyboards

This allows you to activate additional keyboards such as Chinese, Arabic and a number of other keyboards.

International

Choose your Language, Keyboard, and Region Format.

Mail, Contacts, Calendars

This is the hub that lets you set up your email accounts, your contacts and your calendars.

Mail

1 Tap **Settings > Mail, Contacts, Calendars**

2 Tap **Add Account...**

3 Decide which type to use if you know this. You can choose from Microsoft Exchange, iCloud, Google Mail, Yahoo! Mail, or AOL. If you are uncertain, tap Other...

4 Tap **Add Mail Account**

5 Enter your full name, email address and password

6 Give the account a **Description**, e.g. "Work Email"

7 Click **Save** and Mail will configure the account for you. Ignore the **LDAP Account** unless you have been told to configure this by your Internet Service Provider(ISP). You can add **CalDAV** and **Subscribed Calendars** if you need to use these

iCloud accounts
You can configure Mail to switch on Mail, Contacts, Calendars and Bookmarks for iCloud (cloud) syncing. You can also switch **Find My iPad** to ON if you want to use this feature.

You will see the account information displayed under **Settings > Mail, Contacts, Calendars > Name of email account**.

Review the settings for the Mail app
Show – decide how many messages you want to show

Preview – how many lines of the email do you want to preview?

Minimum font size – set the font size for your emails

Hot tip

Find My iPad is now free so set it up and use it if you lose your iPad.

Show To/Cc Label – show or hide this option

Ask Before Deleting – switch to **ON** as a safety measure, preventing the unwanted deletion of emails

Load Remote Images – if an email contains images and you want to see these, switch to **ON**

Always Bcc Myself – for blind copies sent to yourself

Signature – decide what signature you want to appear at the end of each email

Default Account – decide which account should be the default for creating new emails

Contacts

There are few settings to configure here, since the app is very straightforward.

Sort Order – how do you want your contacts listed? By first name or surname?

Display Order – best to use **First, Last**

Default Account – which email account you wish to use as your primary address book

Calendars

New Invitation Alerts – switch to **ON** if you wish to receive these

Sync – what do you want to sync? All events? Two weeks back? Set this option here

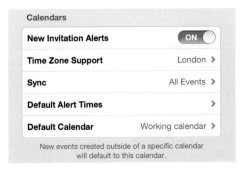

Time Zone Support – set the time zone here

Default Calendar
– determines which calendar is used for new appointments

Twitter
Add your Twitter account and import your Twitter contacts.

Safari settings
Adjusting settings here is like using Preferences or Options on the computer version of the Safari web browser.

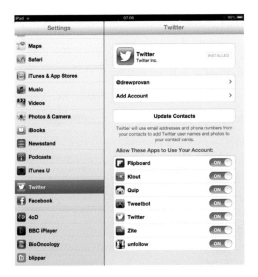

Tap **Settings > Safari**

Search Engine – choose from Google, Yahoo! or Bing

Autofill – use your contact information, since this will include postal address, telephone number and other details

Names and Passwords – if you want Safari to remember your passwords for sites you visit regularly – set to **ON**

Hot tip

Autofill is useful and saves you having to type your personal details on websites.

Always Show
Bookmark Bar – when you want to hide the bookmark bar (why would you?) switch this to **OFF**

Fraud Warning – it is wise to be alerted when you visit potentially fraudulent sites so leave this **ON**

JavaScript – best left **ON** (default)

Block Pop-ups – leave **ON** to avoid annoying pop-ups

Accept Cookies – many sites insist on this but you can clear all the cookies later

Databases – this will list the databases for your Google accounts, Apple User Guides. Ignore this setting

Privacy – here you have the option of clearing your browsing History, Cookies, and Cache

Music Settings (previously iPod settings)
iTunes Match – any music on your iPad that is on iTunes is automatically added to iCloud so you can listen to it on any device

Sound Check – this evens out the volume so that tracks will play back at the same volume

EQ – sets the equalizer which enhances the audio output

Volume Limit – prevents hearing damage by limiting the volume of playback, keeping it at a safe level

Video settings

Start Playing – the default is sensibly set to **Where I Left Off** so you can stop watching a movie and resume later

Closed Captioning – switch to **ON** to display closed-captioning subtitles where these are available

TV Out – if you intend to hook your iPad up to a TV choose **Widescreen** if this matches your display. The TV signal will need to be set to your country's mode, e.g. PAL for Europe and NTSC for North America

Photos

Play Each Slide For – decide how long you want pictures to be displayed during the slideshow. The default is three seconds but you can choose up to 20 seconds

Repeat – do you want the slideshow to repeat? If so, set this to **ON**

Shuffle – switch to **ON** if you want to show the pictures in a random manner

...cont'd

FaceTime settings

Enter the email address you want to use with FaceTime. If you don't want to be contacted using FaceTime you can switch it off.

Store

This is where you set up your account details for the iTunes Store.

Tap **View Account** to see your details, including address, phone number, and credit card.

Hot tip

Setting up iBooks alerts is not obvious. To set up alerts go to **Settings > Store** then tap **Apple ID**. Then tap **View Apple ID**. Sign in with your password and scroll down to **My Alerts**. Set up your alerts from the options shown.

4 Browsing the Web

Browsing the web is probably the most popular activity on desktop and laptop computers so it comes as no surprise that the same is true of the iPad. Safari is preinstalled on the iPad and is a clean, fast browser comparable with Safari on Macs and PCs.

Launching Safari

Safari is the default web browser on the iPad. The app feels similar to Safari on Mac and PC. It has a great interface, and is fast and easy to use. You can do most things on the iPad version apart from download files.

- Safari is on the dock at the bottom of the iPad screen by default. You can move it off the dock but you cannot delete it

- Tap its icon to launch Safari

Anatomy of Safari window

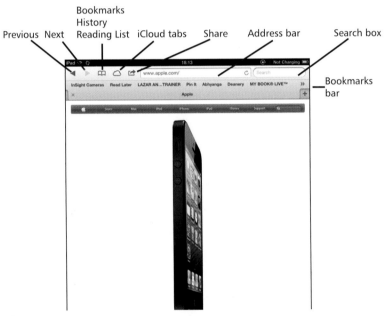

Hot tip

The latest version of Safari includes tabbed browsing. This allows you to switch between pages quickly by touching the appropriate tab.

To open a new page

1. Tap Active Pages icon

2. All open web pages are shown on the screen

3. Remove web pages you no longer want to display by tapping the **X** at the top left corner of each page

4. To open a new web page tap the New Page icon (dotted rectangle)

Browsing Web Pages

Finding web pages using a search engine

- Safari has a search box at the top right of the screen

- Google is the default search engine but you can switch to Yahoo! or Bing if you prefer

- Enter your search terms into the search box

- Tap search on the keyboard (notice the Enter/Return key has changed its name to **Search**)

Navigate to web page if you know the address

The box to the left of the search box is the Address Field. You can type URLs here. Don't worry about typing *http://www*, Safari can figure this out for itself.

1 Enter your URL

2 Tap **Go**

3 Safari will navigate to the web page

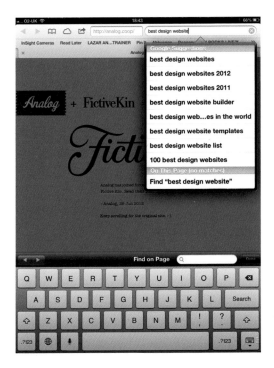

Save Your Pages: Bookmarks

Bookmarks can help you navigate quickly to your favorite sites.

1 Tap to load your saved bookmarks and a list containing all of your bookmarks will drop down

2 Tap on a folder to navigate to the bookmarks inside (if you have folders) or tap a bookmark on the list

Adding new bookmarks

1 Navigate to a site you want to add as a bookmark and Tap the + icon on the toolbar

2 A dropdown menu will appear with **Add Bookmark, Add to Home Screen, Mail Link to this Page**

3 **Add Bookmark** – this adds a bookmark to your list

4 **Add to Home Screen** – adds a shortcut to the iPad screen, making it look like an app

5 **Mail Link to this Page** – to email the link, tap this option

Safari Reader
Add pages to Safari Reader to read later.

Safari History

All of your browsing will leave a history trail behind. This is useful if you want to revisit sites (*you should have saved a bookmark!*). Over time, the history list will become huge so it's a good idea to clear this from time to time. In addition, other people using your iPad can see your history and there may be sites you visit which you would prefer to keep private!

Clear the history

1 Go to **Settings > Safari**

2 Tap **Clear History**

3 You will be asked to **Confirm** this action

4 Tap **Yes** and the history will be cleared

Add Links to Home Screen

The various iPad screens are home to all of your apps, but you can also add web pages as buttons to the Home Screen to make finding and opening these easier. You wouldn't want all of your saved websites to be added to the Home Screen or you would have no room for actual apps. But for websites that are very important, or that you visit regularly, consider adding them to the Home Screen.

1. Navigate to a site you want to save

2. Tap **+**

3. Choose **Add to Home Screen**

4. Name the saved link

5. The web page will resemble an app on the Home Screen

6. Tap it and it will open Safari and take you straight to the correct web page

Safari Privacy

We have already looked at the History and clearing this from time to time. The other item worth clearing on the iPad (and regular computer browsers, for that matter) is the cookies file. This is a file containing sites you have visited and the entries are made by the sites themselves. They don't necessarily do any major harm but for reasons of privacy it is a good idea to clear cookies periodically.

1 Go to **Settings > Safari** – Tap **Clear Cookies**

2 That's it! The cookie list is now empty

Hot tip

For peace of mind, clear Cookies and Cache from time to time.

85

Clearing the cookies

Other Web Browsers

Safari is the default pre-installed browser on the iPad but there others which include:

- Opera Mini (*shown below*)

- Atomic Web

- Privately

- Mercury Web Browser

- Safe Browser

- Browser plus

Some of these are written specifically for the iPad while others are for the iPhone but can be used on the iPad.

What are the advantages of using third-party browsers?

- Many offer private browsing (no history retained)

- If you get bored with Safari and fancy a change try out one of these other ones and see if it suits your needs better

5 Mail

Love it or loathe it, email is a fact of life. We need to deal with email at work and at home. Mail on the iPad makes reading and sending emails a pleasure and in this chapter we will look at how to set up your accounts, manage your Inbox, and make the most of IMAP email.

What is Mail?

We spend much of our time on PCs and Macs checking and sending emails. This is true also of mobile devices like the iPhone, BlackBerry and other handhelds. So, not surprisingly, a fair amount of your time on the iPad will be spent doing emails.

The Mail app built in to the iPad is a feature-rich program that is easy to set up and use. It is similar to Mail, which comes with every Mac PowerBook and Mac desktop, although a few features are lacking. There's no stationery option on the iPad version and you can't have multiple signatures.

Setting up an Email Account

1   Go to **Settings > Mail, Contacts, Calendars**

2   You will see a list of options

3   Choose the one that matches your email account

4   If you can't see it select **Other** – enter your details including email address and password. The program will work out the rest for you

POP or IMAP?

For most people these are fairly confusing terms but it's worth having a look at both types before setting your accounts up. POP stands for *Post Office Protocol* and IMAP means *Internet Message Access Protocol*. These are the two most common standards for email retrieval. POP3 is the current version of POP and is used for web-based email such as Google Mail. Rather than look at the nuts and bolts of these two systems we can summarize the pros and cons of each.

Hot tip

For Mail, IMAP email offers many advantages over POP3.

IMAP lets you see all of your emails using any machine

If you use multiple computers – including handhelds such as BlackBerry or iPad, IMAP allows you to see your various mail folders from any device. The folder structure and the emails within the folders are the same because the folders and emails are kept on a central server (*not* on your computer or iPad).

When you set up a POP3 account you will see folders for Inbox, Sent Mail, Trash but no subfolders or the opportunity to create subfolders to categorize and file your emails. But with an IMAP account you can create as many folders and subfolders (and sub-subfolders) as you like and file all of your emails. You can browse all of your IMAP folders and emails on the iPad and transfer new emails into their respective folders, just as you would with paper mail using a file cabinet. There is a downside to IMAP though – since the emails are stored on a server which may be in the US (iCloud emails are stored in California) if you have no Internet connection you may not be able to see your emails.

So, which should you use?

If your email provider, e.g. Apple (iCloud), provides IMAP then select that. If POP3 is the only option you have, there's not much you can do to change this. For those of us wishing to archive emails and retrieve them months or years later IMAP is the best possible solution.

Composing an Email

① Open **Mail** by tapping its icon and decide which account you want to use (if you have more than one) by tapping **Accounts** and choosing the one you want to use

② Tap the **new email** icon ☑

③ Enter the name of the recipient. As you start typing, Mail will present you with a list of possible options. Choose the recipient from the list if it's there

④ Tap the **Subject** box and enter subject here

⑤ Tap the main body of the email and type the text of your email

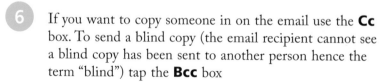

Type (or use Voice Dictation – see icon to left of keyboard if on Wi-Fi)

Mail will spot mistakes and suggest the correct word

⑥ If you want to copy someone in on the email use the **Cc** box. To send a blind copy (the email recipient cannot see a blind copy has been sent to another person hence the term "blind") tap the **Bcc** box

7 Check the **spelling** – any errors will be underlined with a red dotted line. Correct by tapping on the misspelled word and choosing from available options, or delete the word and retype if Mail does not offer the correct word

8 Once you're happy with the content and spelling tap **Send** and your email will be sent

Attach files to an email

At present you cannot attach files in the same way as you would with a regular computer – there's no real "desktop" or filing system you can see in order to find and attach a file.

You can send files such as documents and photos by email on the iPad, but this has to be done *within* an app.

For example, in the Photos app there's an option to share photos by email. You can email Safari web pages from within the Safari program, and document management programs like DocsToGo allow you to email files from within the DocsToGo app.

Here, a photo has been opened in Photos. To email the photo, tap the Share icon (top right) and select **Email Photo** from the drop-down menu options

This option can be found in many apps on the iPad

Note, you can also share from many apps now

Beware

You cannot attach pictures to emails directly – you need to do it from within an app. But remember, you can paste pictures into an email document so if your email is partly written, close Mail (you won't lose the email draft), go to your picture, Copy it then open Mail and paste the picture in.

91

Receiving and Reading Emails

Emails are "pushed" to the iPad from the email server if your iPad is online. You can tell there are unread emails by looking for the badge on the app's icon.

Manually checking for email

You can make Mail check for new email by tapping the ⟳ icon at the bottom of the account window

Reading emails in portrait mode

If you hold the iPad in portrait mode you will see a separate floating account window listing emails in the Inbox.

1 Tap an email in the list and it will fill the whole screen

2 To see the next or previous email tap the down or up arrows ▲ ▼ or tap Inbox again. Next to the word "Inbox" you may see (3) which means you have three unread emails in the Inbox

3 When reading emails you can: **Move** the email ▣ **Delete** 🗑, **Reply or Reply All** ↩, **Forward** the email to someone else ↩, **Compose** a new email ✉

Reading emails in landscape mode

1 Tap the email you want to read – it will be displayed in the right pane

2 If you want to navigate to other folders in your account, tap the name of the account (top left) and you will see a folder list

3 Scroll up or down until you find the folder you want then tap it. You will then see the emails contained within that folder

4 Navigate back up the hierarchy by tapping the account name at the top

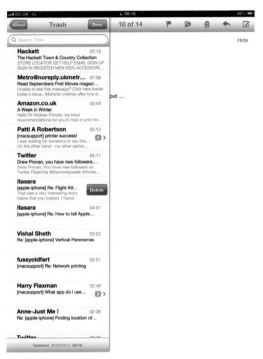

Reading emails in portrait mode – a floating window shows the contents of the Inbox

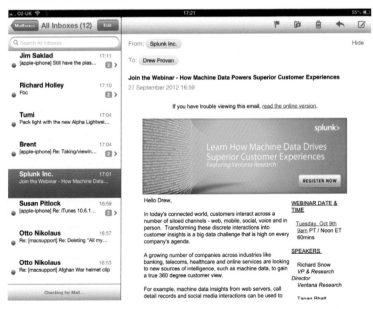

In landscape mode the Inbox sits alongside the open email

Searching for Emails

Mail provides a simple search box at the top left below the account name. You can search: **From, To, Subject, All.**

Searching for emails across multiple accounts

Hot tip

Find emails using Spotlight – don't try to find them manually!

1 Go to **Spotlight** search (press Home Button once or twice depending on whether you are on the first screen or on another screen or an app is open)

2 **Enter your search terms** into the Spotlight search box

3 Spotlight will then search all of your emails (and will search Calendars, Contacts, Music etc. unless you have configured Spotlight so it only searches emails)

4 Once the email you are looking for is listed in the search list, tap it and Mail will open and will take you to that email which will open on the screen

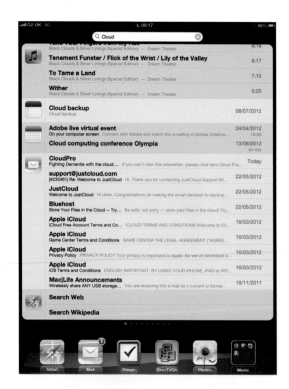

Deleting Unwanted Emails

We all receive email spam or emails we don't want to keep.
It's easy to delete emails, either singly or in batches.

Delete a single email

1 If the email you want to delete is open on the screen,
simply tap the **Trash** icon and the email will be sucked
into the trash folder

2 If you are looking at a list of emails in the account
window, tap **Edit** then tap the radio button next to the
email you want to delete. Then hit **Delete**. The brackets
with (1) tells you that one email has been selected for
Delete or Move

3 Another way of deleting emails is to view the list in the
accounts window then drag your finger across the email
from left → right and a **Delete** button will appear. Tap
this and the email will be deleted

Retrieve Deleted Emails

Have my emails gone forever?

You may accidentally delete an email you wanted to keep. You can get this back!

1   Tap the **name** of the account

2   Tap **Trash**. Look down the list for emails you want to recover from the Trash

3   Tap **Edit**

4   Tap the **radio button** of the email you want to recover

5   Tap **Move**

6   Choose **Inbox**

7   The message will move from Trash → Inbox

Panic over!

Don't forget

Deleted emails can usually be salvaged from the Trash if you want to recover them.

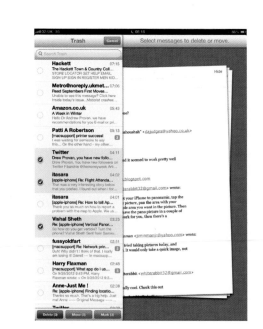

Get Organized!

Filing emails

You should get into the habit of filing your emails.

Create a new mail folder

1 Go to an account and tap **Edit** (top right)

2 Tap where you want the new mailbox and tap **New Mailbox**

3 Name it and Tap **Save**

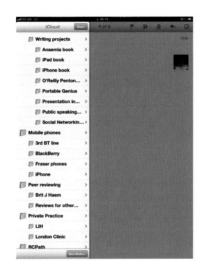

Filing emails

1 With the email open tap the **Move icon**

2 Decide which account you want to use to store the email

3 Navigate to the folder within the account and tap **Move** and the email will move across into its new location

Mail showing all Inboxes and accounts in one floating window

...cont'd

Having selected an email, the Move icon was tapped. The various email accounts are displayed in a floating window. The iCloud account was selected and the various folders are shown below

Flick up and down to see the folders within the iCloud IMAP account and choose the appropriate folder. Once you tap it, the email you have chosen to move will drop into the chosen folder

6 Photos

iPhoto on the Mac is a great piece of software for storing and viewing all of your photos. The iPad app **Photos** *delivers rich-looking photos at high resolution so you can view all of your albums as slideshows or project your photos on a screen or TV.*

Getting Photos onto the iPad

Because of its high resolution display and rich colors, the iPad is perfect for viewing photos. The iPad supports pictures in a number of formats including JPEG, TIFF, GIF and PNG. You can watch slideshows or use your iPad as an electronic picture frame. But how do you get your photos onto the iPad in the first place?

Importing from a computer program

1 You can import from iPhoto or Aperture on the Mac or from Adobe Photoshop Album 2.0 or later, or Adobe Photoshop Elements 3.0 or later

2 Use iTunes to configure which albums you want to sync

3 If you want to remove photos from the iPad, uncheck the button next to the album in iTunes

Hot tip

Another way to get photos on the iPad is to use Photostream. This copies all of your pictures to iCloud and sends copies to your Mac, PC and iPhone!

Using SD Card or Camera

You will need the Apple Camera Connection Kit

1 Plug in the SD Adapter

2 **Insert the SD card** from your camera

3 Click **Import Photos**

4 You will be asked whether you want to keep or delete the photos on the SD card

5 View your photos by tapping the Photos app

Using the SD Camera Connector

1 Plug the SD Camera Connector into the iPad

2 **Attach the camera** using the cable supplied with your camera

3 Make sure the camera is turned **ON** and is in transfer mode

4 Select the photos you want to import

5 Choose whether to delete or keep the photos on the camera

Apple camera accessory (left) and SD card reader (right). To read photos from the card reader, attach the card reader to the base of the iPad, remove the SD card from the camera and slot into the reader. Photos will open and offer to import the photos from the card

Hot tip

For a fourth generation iPad, you'll need to use a lightning to SD card camera reader adapter.

Hot tip

To get photos onto the iPad, the SD card reader is faster than attaching a camera.

Adding Photos from Email

You can email yourself a photo or add any photos you have received in an email.

1 Open the email containing the photo or image

2 Make sure you can see the image you want to import then tap and hold your finger on the image until you see a pop-up saying **Save Image/Copy**

3 Tap **Save Image** and the image will be sent to your camera roll on the iPad

Saving photos or images from Safari web pages

1 Tap and hold your finger on the image you want to save

2 Hold your finger on the image until you see a pop-up saying **Save Image/Copy**

3 Tap **Save Image** and the image will be sent to your camera roll on the iPad

Don't forget

You can save any photos you receive in an email to your Camera Roll.

Viewing Your Photos

1 Launch **Photos**

2 Decide how you want to view your photos

Photos	all photos
Albums	selected albums
Events	selected events
Faces	selected faces
Places	selected places

You need to have chosen to sync Events/Places or Faces in iTunes before these options appear on the iPad.

Viewing albums

1 Tap the **Album tab** to view the album

2 Tap the **Album** you want to view, or pinch and spread using your finger and thumb to spread the photos out

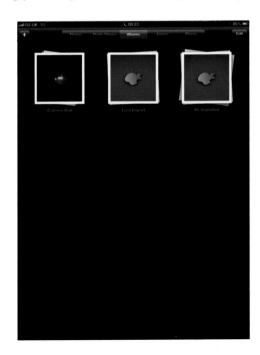

Hot tip

For great editing tools you should check out the new iPhoto app from Apple!

103

Viewing Places

1. Tap the **Places** tab in Photos

2. Tap a **pin** on the map – this displays the location

3. **Pinch and zoom** on the pin to spread out all the photos taken at that location

4. To view a photo at full size, tap it

5. A scroll bar at the bottom shows miniature thumbnails – use this to **navigate** to the photo you want to view

Other Photos Controls

To show and hide the controls

1 **Tap** the **screen**

2 **Tap again** to hide the controls

Tap photo to open

Tap again to see controls

Viewing photos in portrait and landscape

1 To switch to landscape turn the iPad on its side

2 Lock the screen using the software control (slide the Multitasking bar to the right) or use Side Switch

Move through your photo collection

● You can view a slideshow

● Or manually flick through the photos using a finger, flicking left or right

Resizing photos

Pinch and spread using your thumb and finger to shrink or enlarge the photo.

Turning your photos

Use your thumb and index finger – place both on the screen, keep them there and rotate slowly through 90°.

Hot tip

Photos are easy to resize using the pinch and spread technique.

Hot tip

Rotate photos quickly using thumb and index finger. Simply place both on the photo and turn!

Photos Slideshow

1. Tap an **album** to open it or open all your photos by tapping **Photos**

2. Tap the **Slideshow** button (if you can't see the controls, tap the screen)

3. Select a song from the music library

4. Select a **Transition**

5. Tap **Start Slideshow**. If you are showing the photos by connecting the iPad to a TV or AV projector use the Dissolve transition

6. Stop the slideshow by tapping the screen

Emailing Your Photos

1. Open **Photos**

2. **Select** photo to send – **tap** it

3. Tap the **share icon** 📤 and choose email

4. Mail will open with the photo already added to the message

5. Type email and send

Share multiple photos by email

1. Tap **Albums** then tap an album to open it

2. Tap the **share** icon 📤

3. Tap each **picture** you want to send

4. Tap email

5. Enter details and send

...cont'd

Pasting a photo into an email

 Touch and hold a photo or image in Photos, web page or document

 Tap **Copy**

3 **Open Mail** and select New Message

4 Tap inside the email body

5 Select **Paste** to paste the image into the email

Emailing multiple photos

1 Open photo album

2 Tap the icon at the top right ()

 Select photos to email

4 Tap **Share** (top left) and choose email

 The photos will be inserted into a blank email

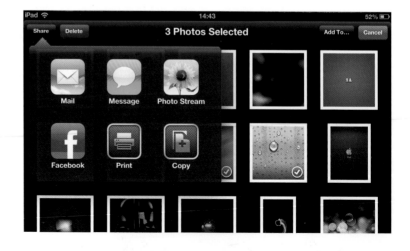

Adding Photos to Contacts

It's easy and more personal to assign a photograph to your contacts.

1 Open **Contacts**

2 Find the contact to which you want to add a photo

3 Tap **Edit**

4 Tap **Add Photo**

5 You will be presented with a photo album and imported photos

6 Select the one you want to use

7 Move and scale until you're happy with the size and position

8 Tap **Use**

Alternative method

1 **Find a photo** and open it by tapping it

2 Tap the **share** icon

3 Choose **Assign to Contact**

4 Choose the contact you want and voilà – the photo will be placed into the photo box for your contact

Use the Inbuilt Cameras

The iPad has cameras on both front (VGA) and back (five megapixels). The back camera is able to shoot at higher resolution (stills and video).

1. Tap the **Camera** icon

2. The iPad default is front camera – if you want to use the rear camera tap the icon

3. Tap the **shutter** icon to take a picture (slide the still camera/video slider to the right if you want to record video)

Tap here when you are ready to take the photo

The photo will be added to the Camera Roll – tap here to open

Tapping this icon toggles between the Front and back cameras

To switch between stills and video slide the button to the right

Use Photos as Wallpaper

Wallpaper, as well as being something you paste onto the walls of your house, is also the term for the backdrop used for the iPad screens. Apple has produced some gorgeous wallpapers for you to use but you can use your own images if you prefer.

1 Find the photo you want to use in photos

2 Tap to open the picture

3 Tap the **share** icon

4 Tap **Use as Wallpaper**

You will then have the option to use this for the Lock Screen or Wallpaper or both.

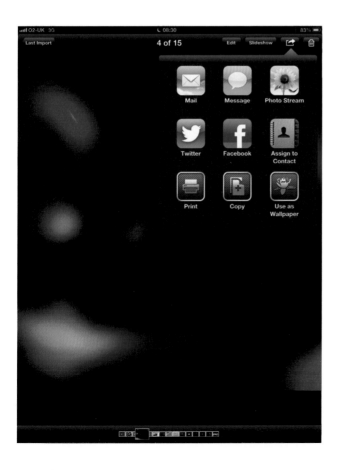

Hot tip

You can use your own photos as wallpapers.

Picture Frame Options

The Picture Frame can be used even when the iPad is locked. Its icon is at the bottom right of the iPad screen when you are viewing the Lock Screen. Adding photos to the electronic Picture Frame show is very easy.

1 Go to **Settings > Picture Frame**

2 Choose the **Transition** (**Dissolve** or **Origami**)

3 If you want the iPad to **Zoom in on Faces** then tap it **ON**

4 To shuffle the order of the photos displayed tap **Shuffle ON**

5 Decide which photos you want to display (**All Photos** or **Selected Albums**)

7 Videos

The iPad, with its Retina Display, is made for video. The high resolution screen and ease of use make Videos a perfect app for watching movies you have bought through iTunes or converted from your own DVDs. You can also record video using the iPad's inbuilt cameras.

Getting Video onto the iPad

The iPad is a great multimedia device for watching movies, TV shows, video podcasts and other video content. The resolution of the screen makes movies crisp and clear. On the iPhone, video content is accessed from within the iPod app but on the iPad movies have their own app – *Videos*.

There are several ways to get videos onto the iPad

- Buy or rent videos using iTunes on the iPad or computer

- Sync videos from the Mac or PC using iTunes

- Using email if the video is short

- Using iPhoto on the Mac (use the Photos pane in iTunes)

- From a folder on your hard drive

Getting your own DVDs onto the iPad

You may have purchased (physical) DVDs and would like to watch them on your iPad. But how can you get them on the iPad? There are several programs for both PC and Mac that will convert DVDs into a variety of formats including iPhone, Apple TV, iPad, and many other formats. Handbrake (*http://handbrake.fr*) is a free app available for both Mac and Windows platforms that makes the conversion so easy.

Hot tip

Use Handbrake to convert your own DVDs for the iPad.

114

Handbrake has an iPad option at present but I use *AppleTV* which looks great on the iPad and Apple TV.

Playing Videos

To play videos on the iPad you need to open the *Videos* app.

1 Tap **Videos** to open the app

2 Tap the **category** you want to watch, e.g. Movies

3 **Select** the one you want

If the video has chapters you can choose a specific chapter to watch.

Where are the controls?

You can use the scrubber bar to move forwards and backwards to a specific place in the video.

1 Tap the **iPad screen** while the movie is playing

2 The controls (**scrubber bar** and **volume**) will appear on screen

3 Slide the **playhead** (filled circle) to where you want to view

...cont'd

The video controls are fairly standard, and are similar throughout iPad apps that play video, including YouTube. The main ones to note in Videos are those that make the screen fill or fit the page. As well as tapping the icons, you can make the video fill the screen by double-tapping the screen while the movie is playing. Double-tapping again will make the video fit (not fill) the screen.

Hot tip

Tap the screen twice when a movie is playing to make it fill the screen. Tap twice again to make it fit the screen.

Pause video	Tap ⏸
Resume playing	Tap ▶ or press center button on Apple headset
Increase/decrease volume	Drag volume slider control or use buttons on Apple headset
Start video over	Drag playhead all the way to the LEFT or tap ⏮
Skip to next chapter (if video contains chapters)	Tap ⏭ or press center button twice on Apple headset
Skip to previous chapter	Tap ⏮ or press center button three times on Apple headset
Start playback at specific chapter	Tap chapter icon then select the chapter you want to view
Fast forward/ Rewind	Touch and hold ⏭ or ⏮
Move to specific point in video	Drag playhead to desired point
Stop watching movie before the end	Tap **Done** or the Home Button to quit the Videos app
Scale video to fill or fit the screen	Tap ⛶ to make video fill screen and tap ⛶ to made video fit the screen
Choose another language	Tap 🗨 then choose language from the Audio list
Show/Hide subtitles	Tap 🗨 and choose language from the subtitle list (if subtitles are available) or tap OFF to hide subtitles
Show/Hide Closed Captioning	Tap 🗨 and tap Show or Hide closed captions (if available)

Purchased or Rented Movies

You can rent or buy movies from the iTunes Store. Also, if you have purchased movies using Apple TV these can be synced to your iPad.

1. Rent or buy movies from the iTunes Store. Allow the movie to download completely (you cannot watch the movie until it has fully downloaded)

2. Tap **Videos** app

3. Tap **Movies**

4. Tap the movie you want to watch

Sync movies purchased on Mac, PC or Apple TV

1. Connect iPad to computer

2. Go to **iPad > Movies** pane in iTunes and check the movie(s) you want to sync to the iPad

3. Click **Apply** then **Sync Now**

Note: The movies you rent *directly* on the iPad cannot be transferred to your computer.

Beware

Movies rented on the iPad cannot be transferred to your computer.

Click the box next to movies you want to sync to the iPad. On this screen you can see three movies have been selected for sync. To remove them from the iPad, uncheck the boxes and the movies will be removed next time you perform a sync

Removing Videos from iPad

There are several ways of taking movies off your iPad

1 Tap **Videos** on the iPad Home Screen to open the app

2 Tap and **hold the movie** you want to remove

3 The **Delete** button will appear

4 Tap the **X** icon to delete the movie

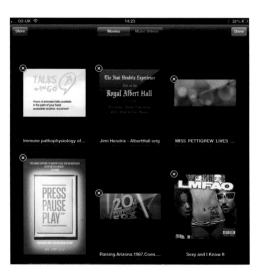

Remove a movie using iTunes

1 With the iPad connected to your computer

2 Go to **iTunes > Movies**

3 **Deselect** the movie you want to remove from the iPad

4 Click **Apply** then **Sync Now**

The selected movie will be removed from the iPad. The movie will *remain* on your computer and if you want to sync it back to the iPad, check its radio button in iTunes.

Watch Movies on TV or Screen

You can connect your iPad to a TV or AV projector. You will need to buy an Apple Component Cable, Apple Composite AV Cable, Apple iPad Dock Connector to VGA Adapter, or the more recent Digital AV Adapter (for HDMI).

Apple iPad dock to VGA Adapter

Apple Digital AV Adapter (allows HDMI output and charging of iPad at the same time)

Hot tip

If you have Apple TV 2 or later you can share your videos using AirPlay wirelessly.

Hot tip

If you have a fourth generation iPad then you'll need lightning adapters.

119

1 **Connect the iPad** to the TV

2 **Select PC** option using your TV's input controls

3 Tap **Videos** to open the app, then select the movie you want to watch

Not all movies can be played

Some movies will not play through the TV – those with DRM (Digital Rights Management) may not play and you may see a warning that you are not authorized to play the movie. The solution (though expensive) may be to buy the movie on physical DVD then run it through Handbrake using the Universal Option, and this should play fine through the TV.

Beware

You cannot play DRM movies on the TV or a screen using the VGA Connector.

What about Music Videos?

Some music CDs have music videos included, or you may buy Music videos on Apple TV or from another source. These should show up in a separate section of Movies (Music Videos).

Play a music video

1 Open **Videos**

2 Tap **Music Videos**

3 Select the video you want to watch

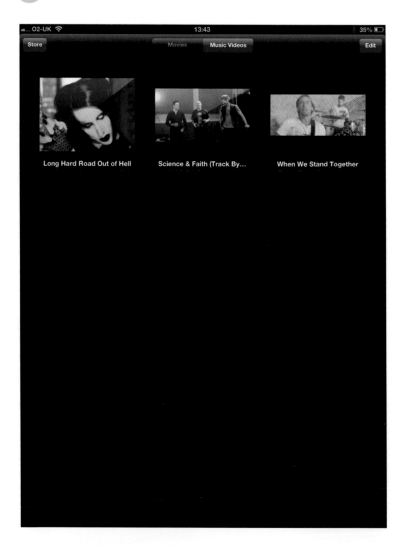

Recording and Editing Video

Recording videos using the iPad is as easy as taking still pictures. Once recorded, you can edit your video and trim unwanted footage, email or send your video to iCloud or YouTube, or share your video by sending to Apple TV.

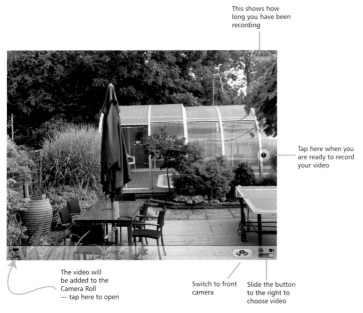

This shows how long you have been recording

Tap here when you are ready to record your video

The video will be added to the Camera Roll — tap here to open

Switch to front camera

Slide the button to the right to choose video

Open Camera app, select Video to record. Tap again to stop

Tap Play to watch the video, or use timeline at the top to edit

Tap the Share button to email the video, send as a Message, or YouTube or make a copy of the video (e.g., to paste into an email)

Share videos using email, Message, or YouTube

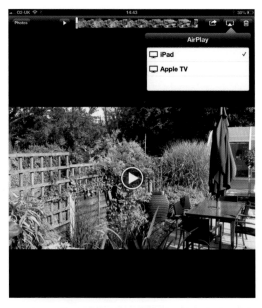

You can share the video by viewing it (wirelessly) using Apple TV 2

8 Podcasts

Instead of storing podcasts in the Music app, iOS 6 brought in a new app specially designed like the App Store and iBooks Store where you can browse and subscribe to podcasts. The app doubles as a podcast audio and video player.

The New Podcasts App

One of the major changes with iOS 6 is the separation of Podcasts from the Music app, where podcasts were stored. Now podcasts have their own dedicated app.

Open the Podcasts app

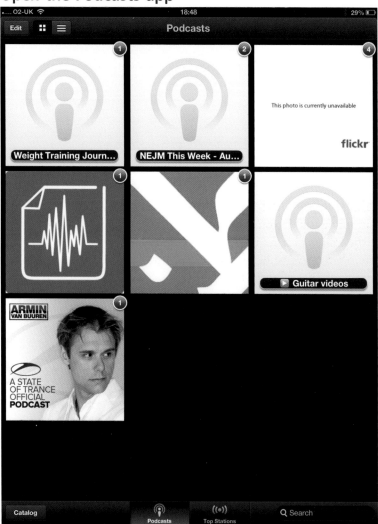

These are the podcasts I subscribe to and have chosen to sync to the iPad. The number of unplayed episodes is shown in the blue circles at the top right of the podcast icon. I can change this view to a list view (*shown on the next page*).

Subscribed podcasts in list view

Selective syncing of podcasts

It is very unlikely you will want *all* of your podcasts on your iPad. In the Podcasts pane of iTunes, select the podcasts you wish to sync. When you want to remove, uncheck their buttons and they will be removed during the sync.

Finding Podcasts

You can search for podcasts from within the Podcasts app or use your Mac or PC (via iTunes).

Using the Podcasts app to find new podcasts

Using iTunes
Use the podcasts tab in the iTunes window to browse podcasts.

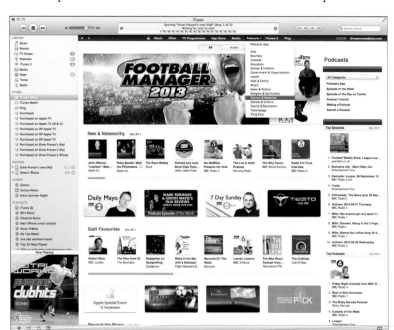

Using Top Stations

A cool feature of the Podcasts app is Top Stations. Almost like using a radio, you can dial up a category and top podcasts in that category are shown.

Here are (audio, note audio/video icons at the top) podcasts in the TV & Film category.

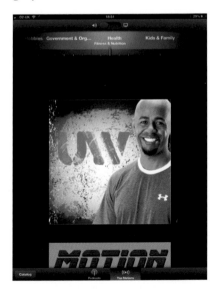

Now we are in the Health, Fitness & Nutrition category, again this is an audio rather than video podcast.

Listening to Podcasts

If you play an audio podcast you hear only sound, while video podcasts play movie podcasts.

The podcast shown above is a video podcast, showing all the usual video controls similar to the Video app.

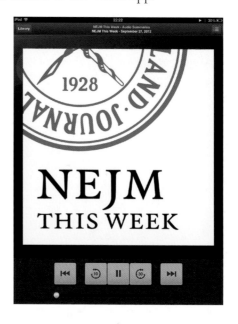

This *New England Journal of Medicine* podcast is an audio podcast.

9 Calendar

You can never be too organized!

Calendar *makes it easy to set up all of your appointments and sync these to your desktop calendar program on both PC or Mac.*

Calendar Navigation

The Calendar app has a clear layout and interface, making it easy to enter and edit appointments. The app is designed to resemble a physical calendar, with a left and right page. Each shows different items depending on which view you are using.

In the **Day** view, the left column shows that day's appointments, with the whole day spread out on the right. The **Week** view shows the whole seven days with all appointments clearly labelled. The **Month** view shows the whole month's appointments, and the **List** view shows both right and left pages with the current day on the right and the list of all appointments (the total Calendar appointments) in the left column. The example below is Day view.

Tap to see various calendars

View by Day, Week, Month, Year or List

Search box

List of appointments

Day view

Tap to go to today

Previous day

Drag the box right or left

Next day

Add appointment

The Calendar Views

You can look at your calendar using **Day**, **Week**, **Month** or **List** views.

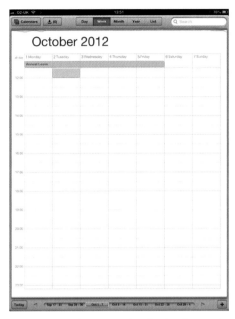

Week view showing detailed information for each day

Month view

...cont'd

Hot tip

The various views are useful for different things – the month is great for an overview but provides little detail. The Day and Week views provide the detail.

Year view: great for an overview of the entire year, but the detail is lacking – you need to use month, week or day view instead

List view: showing a day at a time with all appointments listed down the left page. Flick up and down the left page to see more appointments

Adding Events

You can add events (e.g. *appointments*) to Calendar directly on the iPad or you can use your computer calendar program (iCal on the Mac or Microsoft Outlook on the PC) and sync the events to your iPad.

To add appointments directly onto the iPad

1 Open the **Calendar app**

2 Tap **+** at the bottom right of Calendar window

3 Enter **Title** for the event

4 Enter **Location** if necessary

5 Tap **Starts** and rotate dials to the start time

6 Tap **Ends** (One hour is the default since most meetings last an hour) to add the end time for the event

7 Tap **Repeat** if you want to repeat the event, e.g. anniversary, birthday

8 If you want a reminder tap **Alert**

9 Tap **Calendar** to assign the event to a specific calendar if you have more than one

Hot tip

It's generally easier to add events using a computer especially if you have lots of events to add.

133

Editing Calendar Events

This is very straightforward. Again, you can edit in your computer calendar program or edit directly on the iPad using any of the views (Day, Week, Month or List). Tapping the appointment once in Day or List view takes you straight into edit mode.

1   Tap the **event** to open it

2   Tap **Edit**

3   **Amend** the event making your changes

4   Tap **Done**

Deleting Events

You can delete appointments using your computer or using the iPad. Either way, it's pretty simple.

1 Tap **Calendar** and open the event by tapping it once then tapping Edit

2 At the bottom of the pop-up you will see **Delete Event**

3 Tap **Delete Event** to delete

Sync Calendar with iTunes

You can sync all of your events from your main computer to the iPad and *vice versa* using either wired or wireless options. The wireless method is much more convenient but requires an iCloud account.

Wired Calendar sync

1 Connect the iPad to your computer using the USB cable supplied

2 In iTunes click on the **Info** pane

3 In Sync section ensure Calendar sync option is checked

4 Choose **All calendars** or **Selected calendars**

Wireless sync using iCloud
If you have an iCloud account you have the option of push-syncing events.

1 On the Mac or PC go to the iCloud System Preferences or Control Panel

2 Under **Sync** options make sure the Calendar option is checked

3 Choose the frequency of the sync (Automatically, Hour, Day, Week, Manual)

4 When you add events to Mac, PC or iPad the events will appear on all devices running iCloud

Using Google Calendar

You can add your Google Calendar to the iPad Calendar app. This requires you to set up a new email account using Microsoft Exchange.

The one drawback with this is that you can only have *one* Microsoft Exchange account on your iPad, so if you are already using one for work then you cannot add another.

1. Open **Settings > Mail, Contacts, Calendars**

2. Tap **Add Account...**

3. Choose **Microsoft Exchange** (not Google Mail!)

4. Enter your email address, leaving **Domain** blank

5. Add a **Description** for the account if you want

6. Tap **Next** (you may see Unable to Verify Certificate – if so, just click **Accept**)

7. In the server box type **m.google.com**

8. Click **Next**

9. You will be asked if you want to Keep or Delete the local (iPad) contents

10. Go back to **Settings > Mail, Contacts, Calendars** and tap the account you have just set up

11. Tap **Mail Days to Sync** and **Mail Folders to Push** (choose the ones you want to push to the iPad)

12. Tap the **email account name**

13. Tap **Done**

Calendar Alarms

How can you be sure you don't miss a crucial appointment? You could look at the Calendar app daily or more often and scan through upcoming events.

But an easier way is to set an alarm, or reminder if the event is really important, for example you might want a reminder two days before an assignment has to be handed in.

On the iPad Calendar, reminders appear as notifications (with sound) on the screen. Set these up by going to **Edit** mode then tap **Alert**. Decide how far ahead you want the alert.

You can choose to set the alert for five minutes before the event or you can make it much longer. Unfortunately you can't set it for more than two days beforehand

The alert shows as a notification on the screen (locked or unlocked) and there will be an alarm sound so you cannot ignore the alert!

10 Contacts

*Gone are the days when we stored
contacts just on a cell phone SIM card.
The world of contacts has become much
more advanced and* Contacts *makes it
easy to add and import contacts, making
their details instantly available on
your iPad.*

Exploring the Contacts App

The Contacts app is a simple but elegant app for managing all of your contact information. The app is designed to resemble a physical address book, showing your **Contacts** and **Groups** down the left hand page with contact details shown on the right facing page.

To see Groups tap here

Search box

Alphabetical thumb tabs

Add a new contact   Edit contact   Share contact details by email

You can also browse Contacts in landscape view but the details are much the same as portrait although the pages are a bit wider.

Toggle between Groups and All Contacts

If you have groups, you can access these from within Contacts. You cannot set up a group on Contacts, though – the group itself needs to be created using your computer contacts program.

1 Tap the red marker when you are in **All Contacts**

2 The page will turn and you will see your **Groups**

3 Tap the **red marker** on the right page and you will go back to contacts

Adding Contacts

You can add contacts by syncing with your PC or Mac and importing all of your contacts, or by adding contacts directly onto the iPad (these will sync later to your computer).

Sync contacts from computer

1 Connect iPad to the PC or Mac

2 In iTunes click **iPad** in the left pane (Devices)

3 Select the **Info** pane in iTunes and look for Contacts

4 Choose **All contacts** or **Selected groups**

5 Click **Apply** then **Sync Now**

Your Mac or PC contacts will sync across to the iPad from Address Book (Mac) or Microsoft Outlook (PC).

Yahoo! and Google contacts

To add these click the buttons in the Info pane in iTunes.

Add a new contact

1 Launch **Contacts**

2 Tap the **+** icon at the bottom of the left hand page

3 Enter details into Contact page, adding a photo if necessary

4 Click **Done** when finished

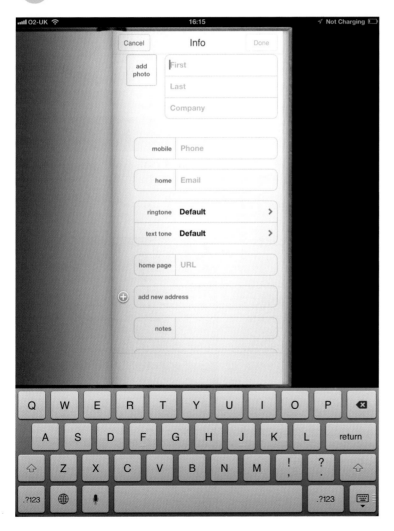

Edit and Delete Contacts

Edit a contact

This is easy and can be done on the computer (changes will sync later) or directly on the iPad.

1 Open **Contacts** app

2 Select the contact you want to edit

3 Amend the details

4 Tap **Done** when finished

Delete a contact

You can delete contacts by removing them from iCal or Microsoft Outlook and when you next sync, that contact will be removed.

Or you can delete straight from the iPad itself.

1 Open **Contacts** app

2 Select the contact you want to delete

3 Tap **Edit**

4 Scroll to the bottom of the contact page

5 Tap **Delete**

Assigning Photos

You won't want to have photos for all your contacts but for family and friends it is great to have their picture displayed in the contact list.

1 Open **Contacts**

2 Find the contact to which you want to assign a photo

3 Tap **Edit**

4 Tap **add photo**

5 Select a photo from the list of photos shown

6 Tap **Done** when you're happy with your choice

Hot tip

Add photos to friends' and family contacts – it makes it more personal.

Sharing Contact Details

You can send a contact's details to a friend using email.

1 Open the Contacts app

2 Select contact you want to share

3 Tap **Share** at the bottom of the right-hand page

Send an iMessage to a Contact

Apple introduced iMessage for iPhone and iPad, and now OS X for Mac. Using your iPad you can send an iMessage if you are on Wi-Fi. If you use an iPhone you can send iMessages or SMS but the iPad only has the iMessage option.

1 Open **Messages** app

2 Tap the **To:** box and enter a contact to message and choose their email/phone number

3 Type your text and add a photo (icon to the left of the message box) then tap Send

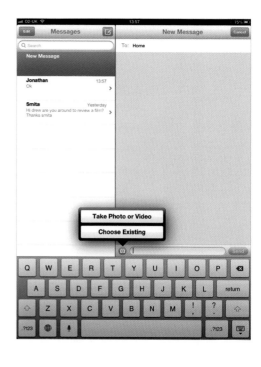

11 Notes

Notes *takes the place of post–its. The app is simple but effective. Not only can you make and store notes on your iPad, you can also sync these to your computer so you need never forget anything again!*

What is the Notes App?

Notes is the simplest of the installed apps. It is much like Notes on the iPhone although the interface is somewhat better. It resembles a tear-off notepad. What you see depends on whether you hold the iPad in the portrait or landscape position.

In portrait mode (left) you can see all notes in a floating window. The landscape mode (below) is more impressive, with a leather holder effect showing the list of notes in a separate 'pad' with the current note being viewed on the right

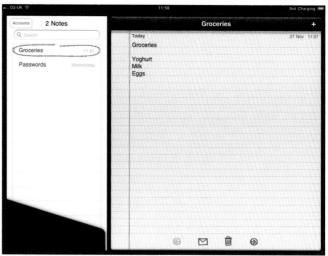

Syncing notes to the computer

The notes you create are intended to sync to your computer. On the Mac the notes sync with Apple Mail and on the PC side the notes sync with Outlook. Notes can be synced using a wired connection with your iPad hooked up to iTunes, or you can choose Notes sync using iCloud.

Adding a New Note

1 Tap the **+** symbol at the upper right of the screen

2 A new note is generated

3 Type in your text (on the first line, enter something that tells you what the note is about since the first line is used as the title of the note)

4 To finish, tap **Notes** (upper left corner of the window) to take you back to the list of notes

5 Your new note will now be in the list and will have a red marker around it

Sharing Notes

As well as viewing your notes on the iPad, you can email them to yourself and to others. You can also send the note in a Message, as well as copy and print the note.

1. Open the **Notes** app

2. Add a new note or open an existing note

3. Tap the **email icon** at the bottom of the screen

4. A new email window will open and the cursor will be flashing in the **To:** field

5. **Enter the address** of the recipient

6. Tap **Send**

Hot tip

If a note is very important, consider emailing it to yourself.

Note sharing options

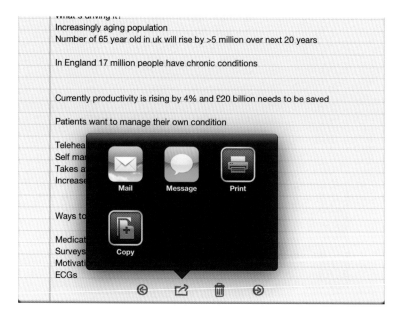

Syncing Notes

This feature still has some bugs. In theory, if you have an iCloud account your notes *should* sync via the cloud to your Mac or PC, and also to your iPhone but syncing is not 100% reliable. Notes on the iPad will sync with Apple Mail on the Mac and Microsoft Outlook 2003 or 2007 on the PC.

iCloud sync

1 Open **iCloud** on your Mac or PC (System Preferences on the Mac or Control Panel on the PC)

2 Click the **Sync** tab

3 Ensure **Mail & Notes** has a check mark against it

4 In theory, any note you create on the Mac or PC should sync to iCloud in the cloud and end up on your iPad. It works well for the iPhone but not as well on the iPad

iTunes sync

1 Connect your iPad to your computer

2 Open iTunes and select **Info pane**

3 Scroll all the way down to the bottom and you should see **Advanced**

4 Check the Notes box if you want iTunes to sync your notes

Hot tip

Your notes can be synced between the iPad and your computer.

Can You Change Notes Font?

Until iOS 4.2 it was difficult to change the font from Marker Felt to any other but now we have the option of using one of three typefaces: Noteworthy, Helvetica, and Marker Felt. Helvetica is the most neutral of the fonts – the other two are not liked by many people. Marker Felt looks too unbusinesslike!

Changing the Notes font

1 Go to **Settings** > **Notes**

2 Choose the default font for all notes

12 Maps

Maps *makes it easy to locate yourself, find places, gauge traffic conditions and get directions to anywhere – on foot, by car and using public transport. There are a few glitches in the iOS 6 Maps app but these should be ironed out with iOS 6 updates.*

What is Maps?

If you have an iPhone you will be familiar with Maps since the iPad version is pretty similar although much enhanced. The app uses Tom Tom as its engine, and shows you a map of where you are, what direction you are facing, street names, directions to a given place from where you are currently (walking, by car and by public transport), and traffic.

The iPad version's large screen shows several views:

- Classic

- Satellite

- Hybrid

- Terrain

To use Maps you will need an active Internet connection – either Wi-Fi or 3G/4G.

Beware

You need an active network connection to use Maps.

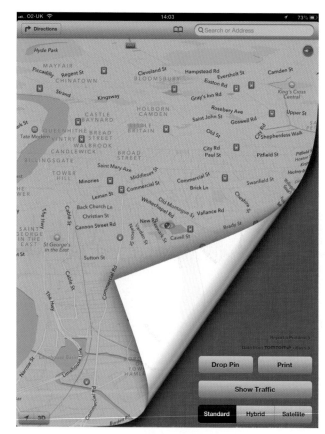

The Maps Views

There are four views, each showing slightly different detail. Classic is probably the most useful since it shows the typical A-Z style of map layout.

Classic view – stylistic but very functional

Satellite view – as the name suggests is a satellite image of the area

Hot tip

Although less glitzy, the Classic view is the most practical.

Hybrid view – combines the satellite detail with street names overlaid

Satellite 3D view – showing parks, water and other terrain

Finding Places

You can find a location using a number of methods

- Address
- By intersection
- Area
- Landmark
- Bookmark
- Contact
- ZIP/postal code

To find a location

1 Tap the **Search field** to show the keyboard

2 Enter the address or other search information

3 Tap **Search**

4 A pin will drop onto the map showing location

5 Google My Maps will display places of interest nearby

Zoom in and out

Zoom in	Pinch map with thumb and forefinger and spread apart or double-tap with one finger to zoom in
Zoom out	Pinch map with thumb and forefinger and bring together or tap with two fingers to zoom out
Pan and scroll	Drag the map up, down, left or right

Your Current Location

Find your current location

1 Tap the **map** quickly

2 A compass will show the direction you are facing

3 Your **location** is shown as a blue marker

The digital compass

 Compass icon, but compass is black which means it is not active

 Tap the compass icon and it turns blue and now shows North

 Tap again and this icon points to show you the direction you are facing

Hot tip

Tap the compass to find out which direction you are facing. May save you having to do a U-turn!

157

Want to know more about your current location?

1 Tap the **blue marker**

2 Tap the (**i**) symbol

3 Details of your location will be displayed

Current Location
The Royal London Hospital, 2 Turner Street, Poplar, E1 2AE, England

Marking Locations

How to mark locations

You can drop pins onto the map for future reference.

 Touch and hold any location to drop a pin

Touch and hold then **drag the pin** to the desired location

To save it, tap the (**i**) icon and then tap **Add to Bookmarks**

Hot tip

Marking locations is very easy – just touch and hold your finger on the screen to drop a pin.

That pin will serve as a marker for future use

To see your dropped pin locations tap **Bookmarks**

A list of your dropped pins will appear

Tap the one you want to view

Edit your bookmarks

Just like a web browser, you can edit and delete the bookmarked locations.

Clear bookmarks

Tap **Edit** then tap the delete symbol.

To rearrange the order

Tap **Edit** then touch and hold the bookmarks and slide up and down to the desired location.

Editing and reordering bookmarks

1 Tap **Bookmarks > Edit**

2 You can delete bookmarks

3 Reorder them by holding the right side and moving to new position

Information about a location
Touch the pin and a window will pop up.

Get Directions

Directions are available for driving, public transport, and walking

1   Tap **Directions**

2   **Enter** the **Start** and **End** locations into the boxes at the top of the screen

3   If the address is in the Contacts list tap and choose the contact

4   Tap the icon if you want to reverse the directions

5   Choose Directions for driving, public transport, or walking

By car   On foot   Public transport

You can view the directions as a stepwise guide or a complete list

Alternative method for finding directions

1 Tap a **pin** on the map

2 Tap **Directions To Here** or **Directions From Here**

3 **Reverse** by tapping ⇅

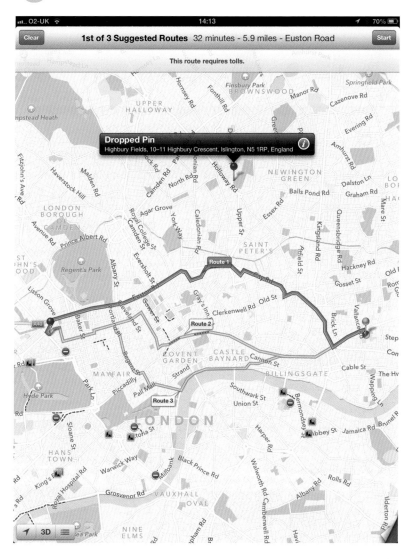

Traffic Conditions

Maps can show you the traffic conditions for locations. (This feature did not work for all countries or cities at the time of printing.)

1   Tap **bottom right of the screen** to flip the page and turn Traffic on and off (or drag the bottom right of the screen to reveal the traffic button)

2   The traffic conditions are shown as colors:

Green	average speed is >50mph
Yellow	25–50mph
Red	<25mph
Gray	traffic information is not available

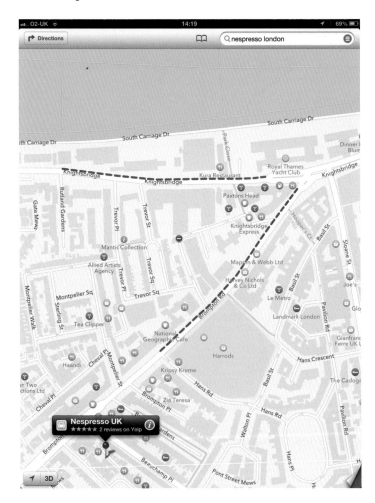

13 Music

The original iPod revolutionized the way we store and listen to music and other audio content. The iPad's Music app is a great music player, and much more.

The Music Interface

This is similar to the standard Music interface on the iPod and iPhone but because the screen is so much larger, the app is clearer and easier to use. You can browse your music by *Artist*, *Album*, *Song* and several other ways. Although the iPad has an internal speaker, the music quality is poor. You need to attach a decent pair of headphones to hear the full quality of the Music app sound.

Beware

The iPad's inbuilt speakers are not very good – for music and video you need to attach headphones.

Since iOS 5.0 was introduced the interface of the Music app has become less usable and there are alternative apps available on the App Store.

Left: standard Music app window showing the Songs view

Below left: Planetary. Visually stunning and free!

Below right: Groove 2. Great for generating mixes when you get bored of your playlists!

By using the buttons at the bottom of the screen you can browse through your music in a number of ways, including by Artist, Song, Album, Genre or Composer.

Browsing your library by Songs – Playlists are shown in the left panel, and all the songs on your iPad are shown on the right

Browsing the iPad by Albums – you can see the cover art clearly

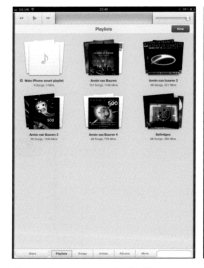

If you have created playlists you can tap Playlists and select the one you want

The Composer view – probably the least useful of all the views. Looks much like Artist view

Music Controls

The Music controls can be accessed from the library window or when you tap the cover art for the current track.

The controls are very intuitive and are much the same as for the standard iPod. If the controls are not obvious, you may need to tap the screen to bring them up (the same is true of most apps – when video or music content is playing on the iPad, the controls fade).

The main controls used to play music are shown below. What you see varies depending on how you are browsing your music.

Previous Play/Pause Next   Scrubber bar   Genius Volume AirPlay

Repeat   Shuffle

Store   Artist view   Search

Pause	Tap ⏸
Resume	Tap ▶
Increase/Decrease volume	Drag slider control on screen, or use button on the right side of the iPad or use volume control on headset if available
Restart song or chapter	Tap ⏮
Next song or chapter	Tap ⏭
Previous song or chapter	Tap ⏮ twice
Rewind or fast forward	Touch and hold ⏮ or ⏭
See full album art	Tap album cover when song is playing
Repeat songs	🔁 tap twice to repeat current song
	🔁 repeat all songs in album
	🔂 repeat current song
	🔁 no repeat
Select point in song	Drag playhead along the scrubber bar
Shuffle songs	Tap 🔀 to shuffle. Tap 🔀 again to play in order
Shuffle tracks in playlist, album or other list of songs	Tap album art to show song controls. Tap 🔳 then tap shuffle 🔀

The Library

You can browse Music, Audio, Podcasts and other Music content in both portrait and landscape modes.

Library in portrait mode

Library in landscape mode

Playing Music

Viewing the Music controls when using other apps

1 Double-tap the **Home Button**

2 Multitasking bar will pop up from the bottom of screen

3 Slide the Multitasking bar to the right to reveal the Music controls

Below is a screenshot from Pages, showing the Music controls on the Multitasking bar.

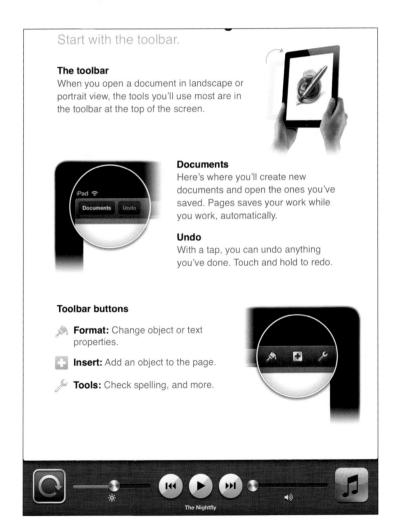

iTunes Store

This is covered in more detail in Chapter 14.

From the Music app, tap Store (bottom left button) and you will be taken straight to the store (you will be taken out of the Music app to the iTunes Store, which is a separate app).

Here you can browse available content which includes:

- Music
- Films
- TV Programmes
- Audiobooks
- Charts
- Genius
- Purchased (items you have purchased previously)

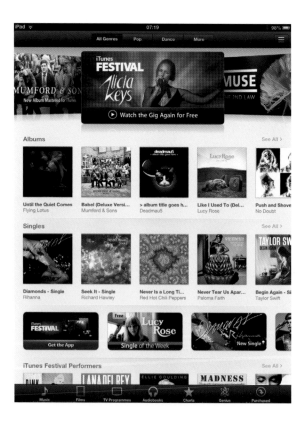

Creating Playlists

This is a great way to collect songs you like into one list rather than having to hunt around for them.

1 Click the **New Playlist** icon (bottom left of the Music screen)

2 Enter a **name** for your playlist then tap **Save**

3 All of your songs on the iPad will be listed but you won't want to include them all!

4 Click (**+**) for each one you want to add

5 When added, the track listing turns gray so you know it has been added to the playlist

6 When you are happy with the selection tap **Done**

7 To edit the playlist tap **Edit** and remove/add other songs, or change the playing order by moving tracks up and down (touch and hold the track with your finger then move the track)

Hot tip

Creating playlists is the easiest way to group your favorite tracks together.

171

Tap + then name playlist

Add the tracks you want

Genius Mixes

Based on the track you want to play, the Genius tool will work out what other tracks would fit well with that track. For example, if you play a jazz track, Genius will suggest other jazz songs from your library that would fit well with the track you are playing.

- You need to **turn Genius on in iTunes** on your computer

- You will need to sync your iPad with your computer at least once

- When a song is playing tap **Genius**

- A playlist of 25 songs will be created, containing music that should match the original track

- Genius playlists will be named after the main track used to generate the playlist

Genius playlist based on the track currently playing

14 iTunes Store

The iTunes Store is a huge resource for music, films, TV shows, podcasts and other media. The iPad version is simple to use so you can browse the iTunes Store and download content quickly and easily.

Welcome to the iTunes Store

This app is a great hub for browsing new music, and renting or buying music and other media including:

- Songs and albums
- Videos
- TV shows
- Audiobooks
- iTunes University classes (directs you to iTunesU app)
- Podcasts

There are more than 20 million music tracks and thousands of movies available for download. Purchases can be made using your iTunes account or redeeming an iTunes gift card.

You will need an iTunes account to buy things from the Store, and for many functions on the iPad. If you haven't got one it would be best to set one up.

First, log in to your iTunes account

1. Tap **Settings**
2. Tap **Store**
3. Tap **Sign In**
4. Enter your **username** and **password**

If you don't have an iTunes account

1. Tap **Settings**
2. Tap **Store**
3. Tap **Create New Account**
4. Follow the instructions to lead you through the setup process

Hot tip

The iTunes Store has >28 million music tracks, >1 million podcasts, and >45,000 movies.

Beware

You need an iTunes account to use the iTunes Store. If you don't have one, set one up!

Layout of the iTunes Store

Search for content

New items

iTunes Store content

Finding content using Categories

Music

Browse music by tapping the **Music icon** at the bottom of the screen.

You can browse

Featured Music	
Top Charts	
Genius Recommendations	These are made for you by Genius based on your previous purchases and the content on your iPad
Genres	Helps you browse music of a specific type, e.g. jazz
Search	Using the search function box at the top of the screen on the right

Hot tip

Genius is a great way of finding new music.

Films

The store makes it easy to browse for movies and to rent or buy these. You can browse by Featured, Top Charts, and Genius.

Search for movies using the search box and Genius

1 Tap the **movie** to open an information window which shows the cost of rental or purchase

2 **Film definition**: standard or high definition (HD)

3 Tap **preview** to see a short preview of the film before you buy

4 **Tell a Friend** – opens an email with a link to the movie, including details about the movie

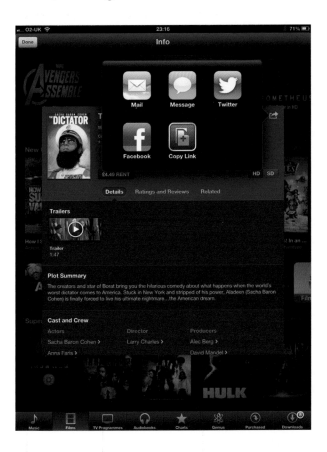

TV Programs

Just like Movies, you can buy or rent TV Shows directly from the iTunes Store.

Browse by

- Featured

- Top Charts

- Genius

- Genres

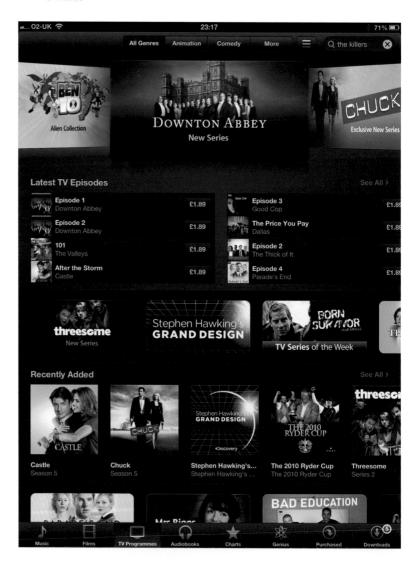

Podcasts

There are thousands of podcasts covering a huge range of topics. Many of these are free.

Search podcasts by

- Featured
- Top Charts

Other sites to see podcast listings

http://www.podcastdirectory.com

http://www.podcastingnews.com/forum/links.php

http://www.podcastalley.com

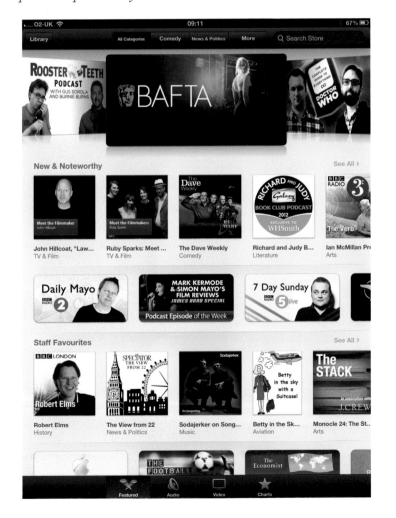

Audiobooks

As the name suggests, audiobooks are books which are listened to rather than read. These are ideal for people who have visual problems.

There are many titles available in the iTunes Store but there are many other sites listing free and paid audiobooks for downloading to your iPad:

- *http://www.audible.co.uk*

- *http://www.audiobooks.org*

- *http://librivox.org*

iTunesU

This is a great educational resource. iTunesU is a distribution system for lectures, language lessons, films, audiobooks, and lots of other educational content.

Finding educational material on iTunesU

Universities & Colleges	Search for content by educational institution (not every university is listed at present)
Beyond Campus	Other agencies offering educational material for download
K–12	Content for Primary and Secondary education. Currently used in the USA, Canada and some Australian territories

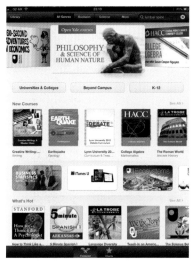

iTunesU is now a separate app. You need to go to the App Store and download iTunesU. Once downloaded, you can decide whether to let iTunesU sync content between your devices. You can then browse iTunesU content

Here is iTunesU in the App Store. Tap **Free** then **Install App**

Genius Suggestions

If you are stuck for ideas in terms of what to buy in terms of music, films, or TV shows you can let Genius make suggestions for you. Genius will look at your previous purchases and make suggestions for you. If you have never bought a TV program using iTunes Store it will say *You do not currently have any recommendations in this category.*

To see the Genius suggestions tap the Genius button at the bottom of the iTunes Store page.

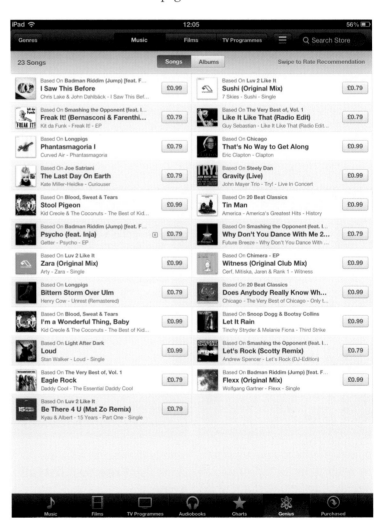

Above you can see songs that Genius has suggested I might purchase.

15 The App Store

The App Store is a vast repository of apps for the iPhone and iPad. The number of third-party apps grows by the day. You can browse and purchase from this burgeoning store right from your iPad and increase the capabilities of your iPad by adding additional functionality.

App Store Layout

You can browse the App Store using the iPad *or* your computer (from within iTunes on the Mac or PC). If you are using a computer, the downloaded apps will be synced to the iPad later when you perform an iPad sync.

Beware

With so many apps available, it is difficult to find new apps easily.

At the time of writing, 400 million iOS devices have been sold and there are 700,000 iOS apps of which 250,000 are for iPad! Overall there have been 30 billion downloads (all iOS apps).

What are the most popular apps?

These are Books, Games, Entertainment, Education and Utilities.

- Tap **Featured** at the bottom of the screen. If it doesn't show, you may not be on the first App Store screen (tap the back arrow icon to navigate to the first screen)

- Tap **Charts** to see the latest apps

- Tap **Genius** to see suggestions based on previous purchases

- Tap **Updates** to update your apps

Featured Apps

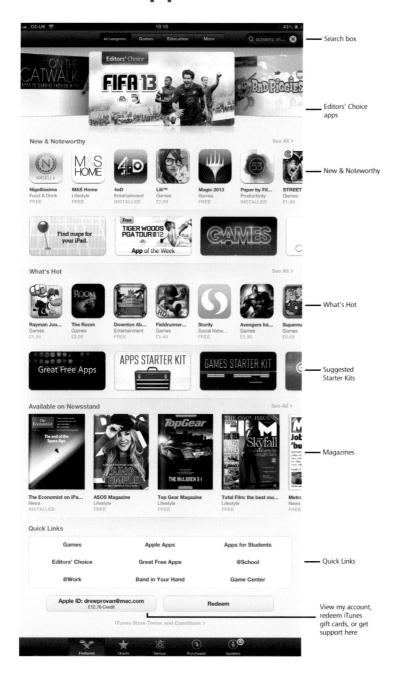

Search box

Editors' Choice apps

New & Noteworthy

What's Hot

Suggested Starter Kits

Magazines

Quick Links

View my account, redeem iTunes gift cards, or get support here

New & Noteworthy

- This will show you the latest apps and those deemed noteworthy by Apple

Top Charts

These apps are the most popular. The screen shows the Top Paid apps on the left side and the Free apps are on the right side.

These are long scrolling lists but if you go right to the bottom and click **See All >** you will then be shown a screen containing Paid or Free apps.

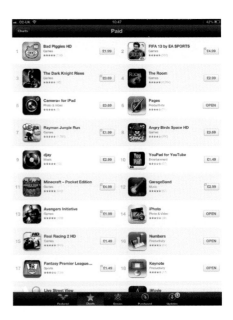

Categories

There are currently 23 categories of apps. This helps (slightly) to find what you're looking for but with more than 700,000 apps, finding an app can be quite difficult! For example, if you tap Lifestyle, you will see more than 2000 apps listed!

As shown on Page 184, it may be easier to browse and find apps using iTunes on your PC or Mac.

All Categories

App Store

All Categories

Games   ›

Education

Newsstand   ›

Books

Business

Catalogues

Entertainment

Finance

Food & Drink

Health & Fitness

Lifestyle

Medical

Music

Navigation

News

Photo & Video

Productivity

Reference

Social Networking

Sports

Travel

Utilities

Weather

Hot tip

There are magazines and books listing and reviewing apps. Consider investing in one of these to help you find useful apps.

187

Genius

The App Store can
make recommendations
for you based on your
previous purchases. In
a sense it "learns" what
you are interested in
and will suggest apps

that fit your buying profile. Sometimes these suggestions are of no
interest to you, in which case you should click **Not Interested**
and the App Store will learn more about your specific interests.

Finding Apps

Standard search methods include

- Knowing what you want! Use the search box

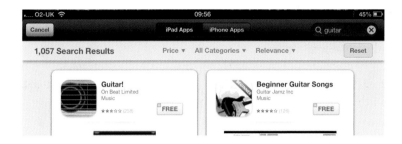

- Knowing roughly where your app is – browse by category

- Browsing using iTunes on Mac or PC. Check the App Store pane to find what you want. You can download on the computer and transfer to the iPad later

Use iPad magazine such as *The Independent Guide to the iPad*, *The iPad Book*, *iPhone Life* among many others. Try browsing websites listing apps such as *appsafari, appcraver, appshopper, 148apps, ipad-application-reviews.com, macworld.com/appguide, appspace.com.*

Buying Apps

1 Tap the **App Store** app to launch it and **Select an app** for purchase. Tap the **app** to open its information screen. The price is shown in gray (if the app is free it will say *Free*)

2 Tap the **price box** – it will turn green and say **BUY APP** (or **INSTALL APP** if free). Tap again to confirm purchase and start download. You will be prompted for your iTunes password. Enter this, and the app will download in the background

Here you can see an app and its price (in gray). After tapping the **price**, the button turns green and says **Buy App**.

Once you tap again, you are prompted for your iTunes password.

Once entered, the app will download to your iPad.

Keeping Apps Up-To-Date

App publishers regularly update their software, ironing out bugs and making improvements. The App Store makes it very easy to see if there are any updates for the apps you have downloaded.

How to determine whether updates are available

- You should see a red badge at the top right of the App Store app icon. The number in the circle tells you how many updates you have waiting to be downloaded

- If you don't see a badge there may still be updates available. Open the **App Store app**, tap **Updates** and if there are any these will be listed. If none is available then you will see **All Apps Are Up To Date**

- You can update one at a time or all at once

- You will be asked for your iTunes password

- Once entered, the app updates will download in the background

Submitting Reviews

Reviews are useful since it may help you decide whether to buy an app or not.

You can submit reviews for any apps you have downloaded (free or paid).

You *cannot* review any app you do not own.

1 Tap the **App Store** icon to launch the app

2 Find the app you want to review

3 In the middle of the screen you should see **Rate This App**

4 Drag your finger along the stars to rate the app between one–five stars (you cannot give any app a zero-star rating)

5 Look for **Write a Review** below

6 Enter your text

7 Click **Submit**

8 You can amend the star rating before you hit the submit button

Deleting Apps

There are several ways you can remove apps from the iPad

- Directly using the iPad itself
- Choosing *not* to sync an app using iTunes on your computer

Deleting directly from the iPad

1. Press and hold an app's icon until all the icons start jiggling

2. Tap the **X** on the top left corner of the app

3. A box will pop up warning you that you are about to delete an app and all of its data

4. If you still want to delete the app press **Delete**

5. Press the **Home Button** again to stop the apps jiggling

The app has gone from the iPad but is still on your computer.

You can resync the app back to the iPad later if you decide you would like to reinstall it back onto the iPad.

Delete from within iTunes

1. Connect the iPad to your computer

2. Open **iTunes > Apps**

3. You will see your iPad screen shown in the right panel of the iTunes Apps pane

4. Find the app you want to delete and hover your pointer over the all until an **X** appears at the top left of the app's icon

5. Click the **X** to delete the app

Don't forget

If you delete an app in the iPad it will remain on your computer.

Syncing Your Apps

This is very similar to syncing other content to the iPad. You can choose exactly which apps get synced to the iPad by checking their boxes in the Apps pane of iTunes.

1 **Connect** your iPad to your computer

2 Open **iTunes**

3 Click the **Apps** pane. All of your apps are listed in a vertical list alphabetically. If the checkbox has a check in it, the app will be synced to the iPad

4 If you don't want the app to sync, uncheck its box

5 Click **Apply** (in the iTunes window, bottom right)

6 Click **Sync**

Creating Folders

As you add more apps you will end up with screen after screen filled with apps. Finding them becomes difficult (unless you prefer to use the Spotlight Search to find your apps). By creating folders, grouping similar types of apps together, you will make life easier for yourself!

How to create a folder

1 **Touch and hold** an app until they jiggle

2 **Drag** an app onto another app

3 A folder will be created

4 The iPad will suggest a name for the folder but feel free to **rename** it to anything you want

Hot tip

Don't like the folder name? Rename it.

Rename the folder

This folder has been named *Lifestyle* but I would prefer to call it *Fitness*. Changing the name is easy.

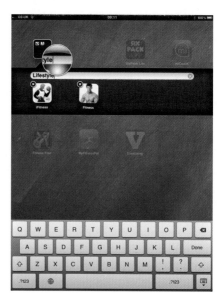

Touch the screen next to the name, insert cursor and rename folder.

16 iBooks

The iPad is competing with some tough cookies in terms of ebook reading. iBooks is an elegant app which lets you browse the iBookstore and save books and PDFs on your bookshelf for reading later. You can read, highlight, use the dictionary, change the appearance of the books and much more.

The iBooks Interface

The iPad is ideal for reading electronic documents including books, and this is a key feature for many people buying the iPad. Just as Apple have made it simple to buy music and other digital content for the iPad, they have done the same with electronic books – ebooks. Browsing and purchasing is simplicity itself. Previewing books before you buy is also possible which saves you buying books you don't want.

The iBooks app provides you with an online **Store** and also a **Library** to store books you have purchased or loaded yourself.

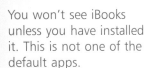

Beware

You won't see iBooks unless you have installed it. This is not one of the default apps.

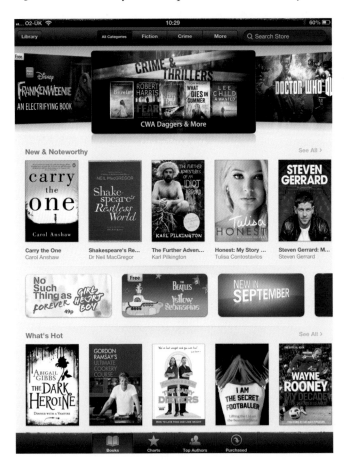

Strangely, the iBooks app is *not* one of the preinstalled apps on the iPad. You need to visit the App Store on the iPad or computer and download the app. iBooks is not available in every country at present.

The library bookshelf

- You can rearrange the books in the Library by tapping **Edit**

- **Move** the books to your chosen position

- **Remove** books by tapping the book you want to delete (you should see)

- Then tap **Delete**

Left: you can browse your collections to see Books, PDFs, etc.

Bottom left: I have tapped Edit then tapped one book which I want to delete. I could tap Delete and the book would be removed but I've realized I've selected the wrong one!

Below right: after tapping edit I touched one book then dragged it to another shelf

Open a Book

Books (ebooks and PDFs) are stored on shelves in your Library. Just like a real library, you can browse your collection, open and read books, add placeholders, and more.

1 Tap **iBooks**

2 Tap **Library** if iBooks opens on the Store page

3 **Select a book** to read – tap to open

4 Choose a specific point to start reading by sliding your finger along the thumbnails at the bottom. The current page is shown as a slightly larger thumbnail

If you close the app or book, iBooks will remember the place and the next time you open it the book will be opened at the same page as you left it.

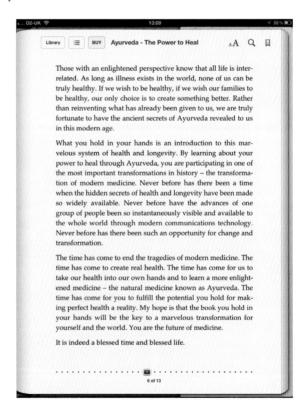

Flicking through a book

1. Tap **iBooks** to open it and **Choose a book** to read

2. Move through the pages by **tapping right or left margins** (moves you forward and backwards through the book). Or you can **touch and hold the bottom corner** moving your finger towards the top left

3. To move to the previous page, touch and hold the left margin and slide your finger L → R across the screen

To move to a specific page in a book

1. Tap the **page** in the center. Controls will appear on the screen

2. Drag the **navigator** at the bottom of the screen to the page you want

Viewing the Table of Contents

1. Tap the page near the center, Controls should appear

2. Tap **Contents**

Add a bookmark to a book

This helps you find your place in a book (you can add multiple bookmarks).

1. While the book is open, touch a word on the page

2. Tap **Bookmark**

3. Remove the bookmark later by touching the bookmarked word then tapping **Delete**

worried
s hidden
a simple

Hot tip

Add as many bookmarks as you want to your book – and remove them just as easily!

...cont'd

Hot tip

The iPad can read books to you (not PDFs, though).

Want the book read to you?

You will need to activate VoiceOver
(**Settings > Accessibility > VoiceOver**).

Highlighting text

You can use highlighters on a physical book to mark specific pieces of text. The same can be done using an ebook.

1 Open the page of a book

2 Press and hold your finger on a word within the text that you want to highlight

3 Drag the **anchor points** to include the text

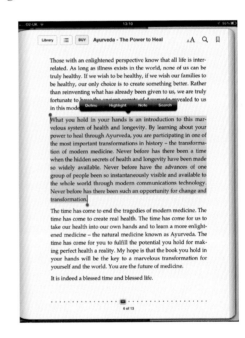

4 Choose **highlight** from the pop-up menu. Your selected text will now have a yellow highlight applied

5 To remove the highlights, tap the **text** again and then select **Remove Highlight**

To select an entire paragraph

Tap anywhere in the paragraph with two fingers. The whole paragraph will be selected.

Using the Dictionary

The inbuilt dictionary is instantly accessible within your books (but not PDF files).

1 Open the page of a book and tap and hold the **word** you want to look up in the dictionary

2 Tap **Define**

3 The phonetic pronunciation and definitions will appear in a pop-up box

4 Tap the page to **close** the dictionary

Hot tip

The Dictionary is not available when reading a PDF.

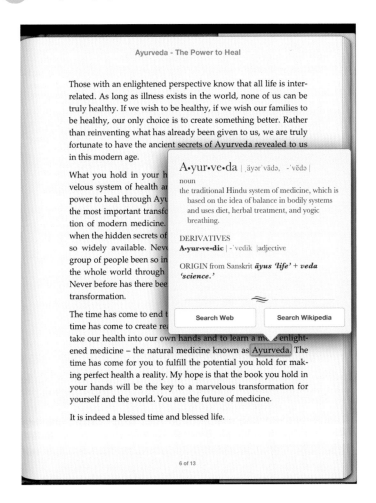

Find Occurrences of Words

You can search an entire book or document for the occurrence of a specific word.

1 Open the page of a book

2 Tap and hold the **word** for which you want to find occurrences

3 Tap **Search**

A drop-down list of all pages containing that word will appear.

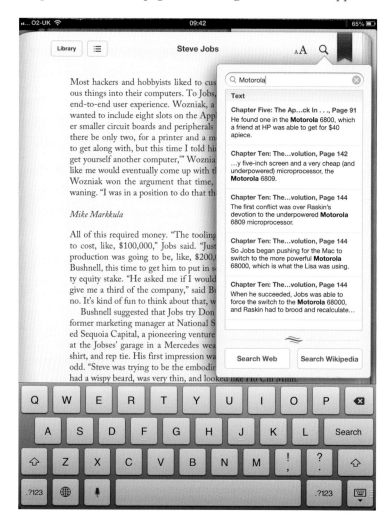

Adjust the Screen Brightness

Depending on the ambient lighting you may need to adjust the screen brightness. For example, if you read in a dark room you could turn the brightness down, whereas outside in sunshine you might need to turn the brightness up.

1 With the page of a book open, tap **settings** (ᴀA)

2 Tap and hold the **slider** to adjust the brightness

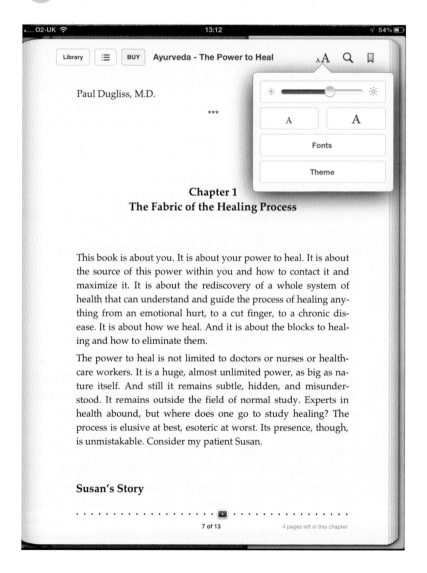

Portrait or Landscape?

The iPad adjusts the orientation of the page depending on how you hold it. If you turn it sideways the pages rotate. This is not particularly convenient when you are lying down.

Hot tip

The side switch on the right-hand side can be configured to either mute the iPad or switch on screen rotation lock (you set this using the Settings options).

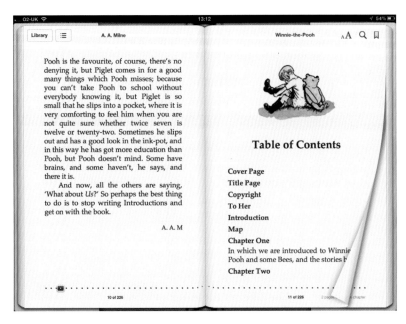

To avoid automatic rotation of the book pages

1. Open a book

2. Hold the iPad in either portrait or landscape mode

3. Lock the screen by activating **Screen Lock** (tap **Home Button** twice to bring up the Multitasking Bar and push to the right)

Hot tip

Reading a book is one of the times when it is definitely useful to lock the screen, especially if you are lying down!

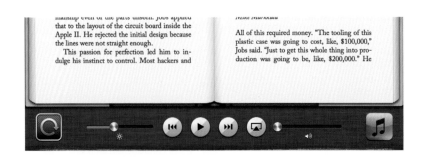

Using the iBookstore

This is a great resource containing many of the popular titles, with more being added daily. The iBookstore is like iTunes except you buy books rather than music, and there is no rental option. Browsing the iBookstore requires an active Internet connection.

Purchased list
This view shows all the books you have purchased (including those titles which are free).

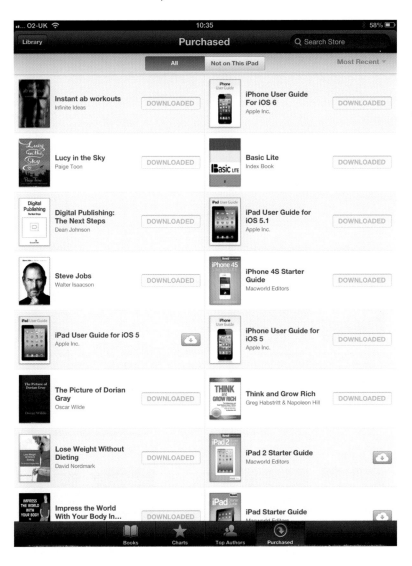

Beware

You need an iTunes account even if you want to download free books.

...cont'd

Browsing is made incredibly easy. You can browse by category or search for specific items.

You can search books by

- **Featured**

- **Top Charts**

- **Categories**

- Typing your **search** terms into the search box

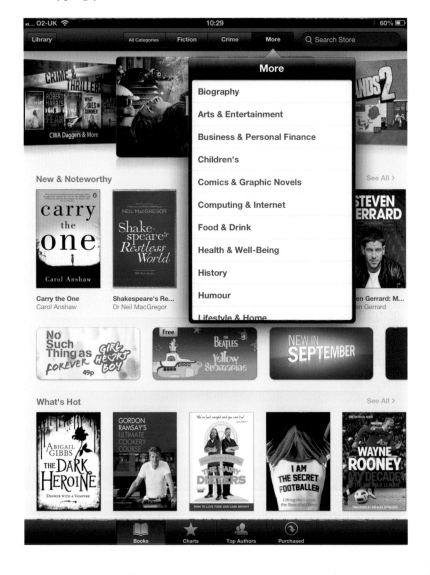

Sample chapters

You can't download music samples in iTunes although you can hear 30 second audio samples before you buy, but you *are* allowed to download short sample chapters of books before you commit to buy. If you like the sample you will probably go back and buy the full title.

Downloading sample chapters

① Open **iBooks** and find a book that you are interested in

② Tap the **book cover** to bring up the information window which floats on top of the current page. You will see *Price, Author Page, Alert Me, Tell a Friend* and *Get Sample*

③ Tap **Get Sample** and this will be downloaded to your library

④ Tap the sample to open

Hot tip

Sample chapters are available for most books so you can try before you buy.

Changing Fonts and Size

Sometimes the font or its size makes it difficult to read a book. With a physical book you cannot change the font but with ebooks you can control the typeface and its size, to make the book as readable as possible.

To change the font or font size

1 Open a book in iBooks

2 Decide which orientation you will use to read the book – portrait or landscape

3 Tap the **font icon**

4 Tap small or large **A** to make font smaller or larger

5 To change the font itself tap **Fonts**

6 Choose from the drop-down list

7 The book pages may have a light brown tint (**sepia effect**). If you like this, keep Sepia **ON**. If you want clinically white pages turn Sepia **OFF**

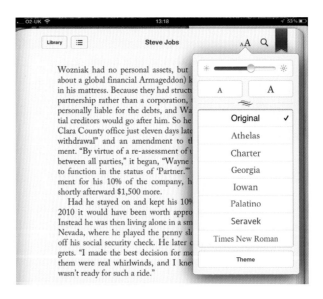

Purchasing Books

Providing you have an iTunes account you can download paid or free books from the iBookstore.

1 Open **iBooks**

2 Tap **Store** if you are currently in Library mode

3 **Find a book** you want to buy

4 Tap its icon to bring up the floating window showing the price

5 Tap the **gray price box**. This will turn green and will say *Buy Book*

6 Tap **Buy Book** (if the book is free it will say *Get Book*)

7 The book will begin to download into your library and the view will change from Store → Library. You will be prompted for your **iTunes password**

8 Once entered, the book will download

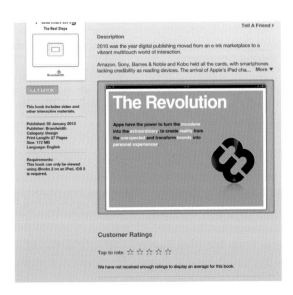

Find More Books by Author

If you have a favorite author or you just want to find more books by the same author you can.

1 Tap the **book cover** to bring up the Information screen

2 Tap **Author Page**

3 You will then see any other books on the iBook Store by the same author

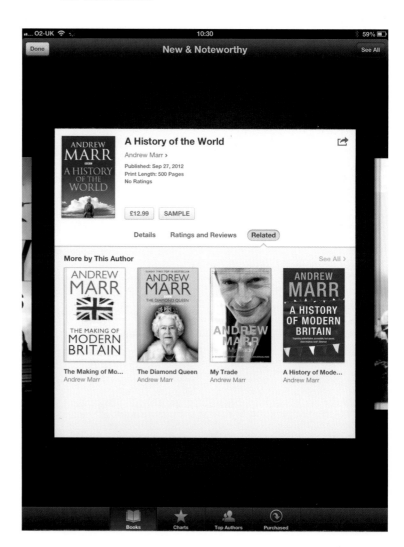

Tell A Friend

You can let other people know about books by sending links to books which they can view on their computer.

1 Tap the **book cover** to bring up the Information screen

2 Tap **Tell a Friend >**

3 An email will open with a link to the book

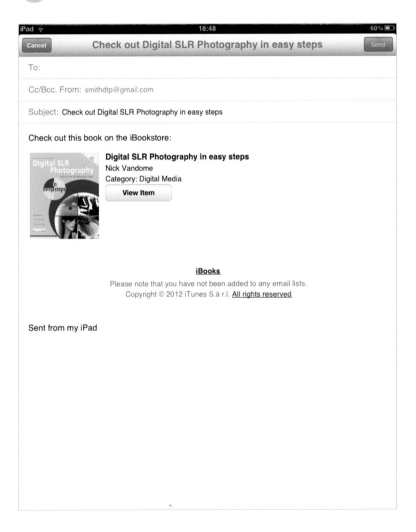

ebooks From Other Sources

You are not completely limited to iBookstore for your electronic books for the iPad.

ePub books

1 Download ePub book (*epubbooks.com*)

2 Add to iTunes (drag and drop the book straight onto iTunes)

3 Connect iPad and sync ePub books to iPad

Other sources for ebooks

- Smashwords (*smashwords.com*)

- Google Books (*books.google.com*)

- Kindle iPad app (*amazon.com*)

- Design your own – many programs allow you to export your files in ePub format, e.g. Adobe InDesign, Storyist, Sigil, and others. Whatever software you use, if it can be saved in the ePub format you can get it onto the iPad. Another option is to save your work as a PDF but you cannot search PDFs for words, or use the dictionary. But it does let you read the document easily

17 The iPad at Work

Sadly, work gets in the way of all this play but the iPad makes giving presentations, writing documents and number-crunching fun! Instead of dragging a heavy laptop to your next meeting, try taking your iPad instead. There's not much you can't do with it!

Storing, Syncing and Editing

The iPad is different to a conventional computer or laptop. There is no "desktop" which means you cannot drag and drop files around and place them in folders, like you would with your laptop.

However, there are still ways of copying files to and from your iPad, allowing you to read and edit text documents, spreadsheets and presentations, and copy them back to your Mac or PC.

There are several apps available that allow you to get files onto the iPad including:

Dropbox (dropbox.com)	Popular on Mac and PC. Provides cloud storage which you can access from any computer. The free account gives you 2 GB storage
DocsToGo & QuickOffice	DocsToGo and QuickOffice essentially do the same thing – they let you read and edit Microsoft Office files. They let you keep local (iPad) and remote (on your PC or Mac) files
iCloud	iCloud gives you 25 GB free storage which is more than MobileMe did previously. The downside is, it isn't a folder where you can drag and drop your files. Useful for keeping things in sync though
Evernote	Useful for storing clippings, web pages, PDFs, Word files and others. The free account provides 2 GB storage and file types are restricted (images, audio, PDF and web pages)

Configure the iPad to view documents

With your iPad connected to your computer, click the **Apps tab** in iTunes. At the bottom of the screen you will see an option for **File Sharing**.

You can configure apps on the iPad to open documents on your iPad. Once you click an app, e.g. DocsToGo, a list of files readable by DocsToGo will appear. Click to select all those you want DocsToGo to open. Then click **Add...**

How you edit your document depends on what app you use on the iPad.

Editing Word documents using DocsToGo

1 Open **DocsToGo** on the iPad

2 Navigate to **Desktop** to add a file from your computer

3 Choose the computer you want to connect to. Tap **My DocsToGo** to see folder contents on the computer

4 Tap the **file** you want to edit (and save locally on the iPad)

5 Once open, tap **Save As**

6 Tap **Location** to navigate back to the local storage i.e. iPad

7 Tap **Local Files**

8 Tap **Select**

9 Tap **Save**

You can now edit and save the file. In PowerPoint you can add notes and edit your slides (in Outline mode only).

Hot tip

Word files can be read and edited easily on the iPad.

Apple iWork Suite

Apple designed a suite of programs called iWork which includes a word processor (**Pages**), spreadsheet (**Numbers**), and presentation package (**Keynote**). The suite has many functions similar to Microsoft Office. All three apps are available as paid downloads from the App Store.

Pages

1. Tap **Pages** to open

2. Select a **document** by flicking through the list from L → R

3. Or **create** a new document

4. Select from the choice of **templates**

5. **Edit** the text

6. Add **graphics** and then tap media – choose illustrations

7. When finished, tap **My Documents** and the document will be saved

8. To **rename** tap the name and enter your own title

9. Tap **Done**

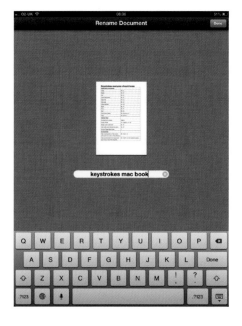

Share documents by tapping the share icon then email, print, copy to iTunes or WebDAV.

Hot tip

Apple's iWork suite is available for the iPad and is very close to the computer version.

Beware

If you use Dropbox to store your word processing documents you will find that although you can open them in Pages you cannot save the changed document back to Dropbox. Annoying? However, for $5 a month you can open a DropDAV account and open and save back to Dropbox. Very easy to set up.

Pages will happily open documents created in Microsoft Word and other formats, and can export in several formats including Microsoft Word.

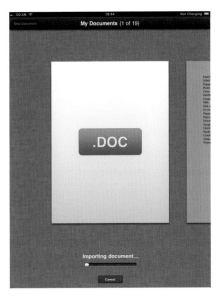

Pages will import Microsoft Word files easily, though some formatting may be lost

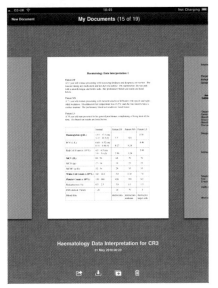

Pages shows you a window containing all documents in the Pages "folder". Flick left or right until you find what you want

Hot tip

Pages can open and edit Word files.

Keynote is Apple's presentation program. It is similar to PowerPoint, although cropping and adding shapes is a bit different. Some aspects of slide design, such as cropping images and creation of shapes, is undoubtedly easier using a mouse but simple slides can be created using the iPad.

Open an existing presentation

1. Tap **Keynote** to open the app

2. Unlike Pages, Keynote only uses landscape mode

3. Flick L → R through existing presentations

4. Find the one you want and tap to open

5. You will see thumbnails down the left side with the slides occupying the rest of the screen

To create a new presentation

1. Tap **My Presentations**

2. Tap **New Presentation**

3. Choose a **template**

4. Tap **+** to add a new slide – a panel showing available Master slides will appear. Select the one that suits your content

5. Add your text

6. **Save** by tapping **My Presentations**

7. **Name** the presentation by tapping its name and entering your own title

8. Save to iTunes or leave on the iPad

Hot tip

Keynote can open
PowerPoint files.

Like Pages, Keynote will open Microsoft PowerPoint files. The
presentation above was created in PowerPoint and saved before
opening in Keynote. Flick right or left to see what presentations
are available

The iPad version of Keynote looks almost identical to the desktop
version. Note the thumbnails down the left margin with the
current (highlighted) slide showing in the main screen

...cont'd

Numbers

Numbers is similar to Microsoft Excel. Data is entered in tabular form and can be used to create all types of charts. Numbers can be used in portrait and landscape modes.

1   Tap **Numbers** to open the app

2   **Enter data** into spreadsheet

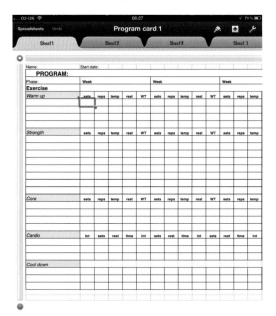

3   Make sure you have selected the correct data type for your columns (**42** = numeric, **🕐** = date/time, **T** = text, **=** calculation)

4   Create **chart**

5   **Save** by tapping My Spreadsheets

6   **Rename** by tapping its name

7   **Save** to iTunes or elsewhere.

Using iPad for Presentations

Just as you would use your laptop to present your PowerPoint or Keynote slides, you can use your iPad once you hook it up to an AV projector or screen.

You will need to buy the iPad Dock Connector to VGA (Video Graphics Array) Adapter. This plugs into the bottom of the iPad and the other end connects to the VGA projector. The iPad can only project certain content – YouTube, non-DRM movies and Keynote.

Present using an AV projector

1 **Connect** the iPad to the projector using the iPad Dock Connector to VGA Adapter

2 Open **Keynote**

3 Choose **Presentation**

The file will open in Presentation mode (rather than Edit mode).

Hot tip

The iPad is great for giving presentations and saves you having to drag a heavy laptop around!

Hot tip

If you have access to an HD display you would be better off using the HDMI connector (Apple Digital AV Adapter).

Editing Microsoft Office Files

You have a number of options, such as DocsToGo, Quickoffice, and a number of other apps to edit Microsoft Office files.

1. **Connect** the iPad to your computer

2. In iTunes go to **Apps tab** and scroll down to File Sharing

3. Click the **app** you want to use to edit your Office files

4. Click the **files** on the right to add them to the iPad

5. Open the **app** you want to use on the iPad, e.g. DocsToGo

6. Go to **Local** to see the files on the iPad

7. Locate document and tap to open OR if you want to open in another app, tap the arrow and choose **Open in...** and select the app from the dropdown list

This document has been opened in Pages, but could just as easily have been opened in DocsToGo natively.

Here is the same document opened in Good Reader, DocsToGo and Quickoffice.

In this example, the document has been opened in DocsToGo. The text is perfectly readable, and can be edited, copied and pasted

Here the document has been opened in Good Reader (a PDF-type app like Adobe Acrobat Reader). The text can be read, copied but not edited

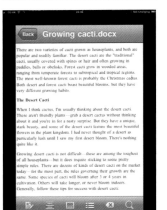

Here we have used the iPhone version of Quickoffice. The iPhone version runs just fine but the size is not optimized for the iPad screen. In order to try to fill the screen the picture has to be doubled in size, resulting in pixellation of the text

There is version for iPad called Quickoffice Pro HD

Get the Latest News

Because the iPad is such a great ebook reader, lots of publishers have made their content available for the web and iPad. This includes newspapers and journals. Many offer free registration, while others have limited content with a paid subscription for full content.

Keep up with politics and economic news

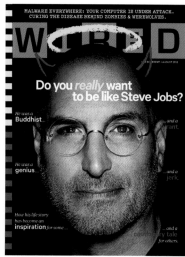

Or tech news with Wired

Medical advances in the British Medical Journal

For the latest in Mac news you can subscribe to Macworld and several other Mac magazines

Get Organized!

We all collect web snippets, photos, PDF files, and other items of information. Finding these on a computer is a nightmare and the iPad has no desktop or folders, which makes it very tricky to store small documents. Try using Dropbox, Evernote or one of the many other solutions to organize your files. You can set these up on your computer then download the iPad version and access all of your saved notes.

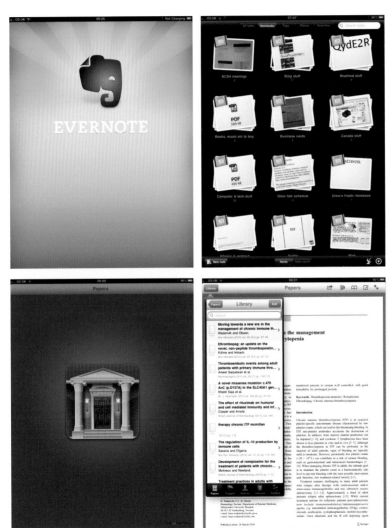

Evernote keeps PDFs, Word and Pages files, web pages, JPEG, TIFF and many other files organized. *Papers* sorts and stores PDF files and is ideal for the well-organized academic

Printing from iPad

The iPad can now support direct printing (called **AirPrint**) but only for a handful of Hewlett-Packard printers. Until Apple releases a fix allowing you to share any networked printer you will need to use a third-party app.

Available apps that enable iPad printing

- PrintCentral
- PrinterShare
- ePrint
- DocPrinter
- ActivePrint 7
- Print n Share

Print web page using Print n Share

1. Copy the web page URL to the clipboard

2. Open Print n Share and select **Web pages** from option at bottom of the screen

3. Paste URL into box at the top then tap the printer icon

4. Print from screen or from the actual web URL (the latter is probably better)

5. Choose your printer by tapping **Choose**

6. Tap **Print**

(18) Accessibility Options

Like the iPhone before it, the iPad has some very effective adjustments which make it easy to use for people with visual and other impairments. This chapter highlights the main accessibility settings which will make the iPad work for you even if you have sight or auditory problems.

Universal Access

Similar to the iPhone, the iPad has a variety of settings that make it easier for people with visual and hearing problems to use.

- Universal Access features
- Playback of Closed Captions
- VoiceOver screen reader
- Full-screen magnification
- White on Black
- Mono audio

Not all features are available for every app. Zoom, White on Black, and Mono Audio work with all apps but VoiceOver only works with the inbuilt apps and some apps on the app store.

Use iTunes to turn Accessibility On and Off

1. Connect your iPad to the computer

2. Within iTunes select **iPad** in the sidebar

3. Click on **Summary** pane

4. Click **Configure Universal Access**

5. Select the **features** you want to use

iPad has many features which make it accessible to those with specific visual or audio needs.

230

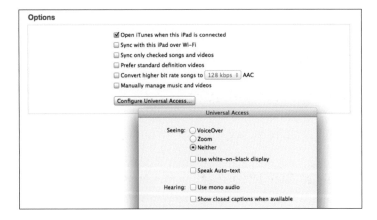

VoiceOver

This setting enables the iPad to tell you what's on the screen even if you cannot see the screen.

1. Touch the screen or drag your fingers to hear the screen items described

2. If text is selected, VoiceOver will read the text to you

Hot tip

If you cannot see the screen text, VoiceOver will read it to you.

To turn VoiceOver On

1. Go to **Settings > General > Accessibility > VoiceOver**

2. Tap **VoiceOver** to turn On or Off

3. Tap **Speak Hints** On or Off

VoiceOver gestures

Tap	Speak item
Flick Right or Left	Select next or previous item
Flick Up or Down	Depends on Rotor Control setting
Two-finger tap	Stop speaking current selection
Two-finger flick Up	Read all from top of screen
Two-finger flick Down	Read all from current position
Three-finger flick Up/Down	Scroll one page at a time
Three-finger flick Right/Left	Next or previous page
Three-finger tap	Speak the scroll status
Four-finger flick Up/Down	Go to first or last element on page
Four-finger flick Right/Left	Next or previous section

Zoom Features

Turn Zoom On and Off

1 Go to **Settings > General > Accessibility > Zoom**

2 Tap **Zoom On/Off**

Zoom in and out

1 **Double-tap** the screen with three fingers. The screen is magnified 200%

2 Increase/decrease magnification – double-tap **three fingers** and tap and **drag** adjust magnification

3 **Move around the screen** by dragging with three fingers

White on Black & Mono Audio

White on Black
This setting completely inverts the iPad colors.

To activate White on Black

1 Go to **Settings > General > Accessibility > White on Black**

2 The screen will now be inverted

Mono Audio
Instead of stereo sound, the Mono Audio channels both right and left output into a single mono output. This is useful for people with hearing impairment, since they can hear the output from both channels in one ear.

Turn Mono Audio On and Off
Go to **Settings > General > Accessibility > Mono Audio**

Speak Auto-Text
Turning on this option lets the iPad speak the text corrections as you type.

Turn on Speak Auto-Text
Go to **Settings > General > Accessibility > Auto-text**

Triple-Click to get Home

You can configure the Home Button to turn the Accessibility features off and on. For example, you might want to use the Triple-Click to switch VoiceOver off and on, or perhaps White on Black.

Triple-click can be configured to

1 Turn VoiceOver off and on

2 Turn White on Black off and on

3 Turn Zoom off and on

4 Go to **Settings > General > Accessibility > Triple-Click Home**

5 Choose the function you want to use with Triple-Click

Index

K

L

M

Q

R

S

T